PAIN RELIEF

Thomas C. Lothian Pty Ltd
132 Albert Road, South Melbourne, Victoria 3205

Copyright © 2002
First published 2002

All rights reserved. No part of this publication may be reproduced, stored in a retrieval system or transmitted in any form by any means without the prior permission of the copyright owner. Enquiries should be made to the publisher.

National Library of Australia
Cataloguing-in-Publication data:

Good, Adrian.
Pain relief.

ISBN 0 7344 0324 0.

1. Manipulation (Therapeutics). 2. Pain - Treatment.
I. Title.

615.82

Cover and text design by David Constable
Cover picture courtesy of Getty Images
Printed in Australia by Griffin Press

Disclaimer
The author has made every effort to ensure that the information contained in this book is complete and accurate. However, the information and advice contained in this book are not intended as a substitute for consulting your doctor or health practitioner regarding any action that may affect your well-being. Individual readers must assume responsibility for their own actions, safety and health. Neither the author nor the publisher shall be liable or responsible for any loss, injury or damage allegedly arising from any information or suggestion contained in this book.

PAIN RELIEF
Manual therapy can help

Dr Adrian Good

Lothian
BOOKS

ACKNOWLEDGEMENTS

This book was written to help people find out about manual therapy, how it all works and how it might be of benefi to them. It also describes the various professions that use manual therapy and the conditions treated by them. It could not have been completed without assistance from many people to whom I am sincerely grateful.

My special appreciation goes to David Tiley, a scriptwriter and editor who appeared out of the blue when I needed him. Without his advice and restructuring the book would not have passed first base.

I am indebted to others from across the manual disciplines who have generously given their time to review all or part of this book. Their contribution has moderated my over-enthusiasm, corrected my ignorance and helped give the balance an individual cannot.

I wish to particularly acknowledge the following friends and colleagues who have provided help and encouraged me to continue: Colin Morley, Peter Bryner, John Murtagh, Jenny Keating, Taj Deora, Peter Gibbons, Victor Wilk, John Reggars, David Vivian, Nigel Mitchell, Anne Ellison and Nick Handoll. They are all leaders in the manual professions and their sound judgement and sensible advice has left its mark on the book.

Peter Lyell, a journalist, dusted down the manuscript and told me how to attract a publisher that had already turned it down. Janet Rowe helped me understand the publishing world. Lara Cubis and Steven Dell, both graphic artists, have provided the anatomical drawings and cartoons that lighten the tome.

I apologise in advance for any opinions given in the text that colleagues and those knowledgeable about manual therapy may disagree with, along with any misconceptions I may have conveyed or just plain errors I have made. I take full responsibility for these — they are not intended to offend, nor are they the fault of others. Despite my best intentions it is not always possible to give readers helpful advice while avoiding every possible sticky area of dispute. Readers are most welcome to communicate their comments and corrections to the publisher.

Finally, it is my special privilege and fortune to have shared my life with my wife Paula. She is the most generous, optimistic and exceptional person I know. Our dear and wonderful children, Jolyon and Lara, have her handle on life to help guide their way. Thank you, as I've never said it before.

Adrian Good

CONTENTS

INTRODUCTION 1
- The purpose of the book ■ The basic techniques
- The question of safety

PART 1
WHAT IS MANUAL THERAPY AND HOW CAN IT HELP? 7

1 BODY MECHANICS 8
- The basic insight ■ How mechanical disorders develop ■ How manual therapy works ■ Where does the pain come from? ■ The pain–spasm–pain cycle ■ Collagen, the body's glue ■ Predisposing conditions ■ Advantages of manual therapy

2 SOFT TISSUE DIAGNOSIS 32
- The soft tissues and their design ■ The rest of the body framework ■ Diagnosis

3 SYMPTOMS AT A DISTANCE 46
- Trapped nerves ■ Referred pain ■ Reflex effects ■ Functional disorders ■ The role of manual therapy in symptoms at a distance ■ Mechanical disorders and medical diseases ■ Is there more to manual therapy?

4 RESPONSES TO TREATMENT 61
■ Reactions ■ Unusual reactions ■ Progress in long-standing problems ■ Scepticism isn't always healthy ■ Minimising reactions

5 BONES AND JOINT CRACKING 69
■ The great 'bone out of place' controversy ■ The question of joints ■ Why is the explanation still current? ■ The crack ■ A variety of diagnoses

6 METHODS OF TREATMENT 81
■ Massage ■ Articulation (stretching) ■ Mobilisation ■ Manipulation ■ Adjustment ■ Exercise ■ Traction ■ Shiatsu, acupressure and trigger points ■ Muscle energy technique ■ Cranial manual therapy ■ Activator technique ■ Applied kinesiology

7 WHO ARE THE MANUAL PRACTITIONERS? 97
■ Bonesetters ■ Massage ■ Osteopathy ■ Chiropractic ■ Manual medicine ■ Manual physiotherapy

8 DIFFERENCES BETWEEN THE BRANCHES 110
■ Massage ■ Osteopathy ■ Chiropractic ■ Manual medicine ■ Manual physiotherapy

9 DEBATES ABOUT MANUAL THERAPY 123
■ Unproven science ■ Education ■ Claims ■ The placebo effect ■ Dangers ■ Unprofessional behaviour ■ X-rays ■ The current medical attitude

PART 2
A GUIDE TO SYMPTOMS AND WHAT THEY MIGHT MEAN 135

10 GENERAL MECHANICAL DISORDERS 136
■ Cracking joints ■ Growing pains ■ Muscle spasm (hypertonia) ■ Osteoarthritis ■ Rheumatism ■ Soft tissue injury ■ Subluxation

11 GENERAL DISORDERS OF THE SPINE 147
■ Intervertebral disc problems ■ Disc sprain

■ Disc prolapse ■ Disc degeneration ■ Intervertebral joint strain ■ Postural strain ■ Pregnancy and the back ■ Scoliosis ■ Spondylosis

12 HEAD SYMPTOMS 166

■ Ear symptoms ■ Eye symptoms ■ Migraine ■ Post-traumatic headache ■ Psychological symptoms ■ Sinus pain ■ Snoring ■ Temporomandibular (jaw) joint disfunction ■ Tension headache ■ Vertigo

13 NECK PAIN 187

■ Acute torticollis ■ Brachial neuritis ■ Cervical ribs ■ Whiplash

14 THE THORACIC SPINE AND CHEST 194

■ Abdominal functional disturbance ■ Chest wall pain ■ Heavy arm syndrome (T3 syndrome) ■ Oesophageal (gullet) pain ■ Respiratory restriction ■ Scheuermann's disease

15 THE LOWER BACK 204

■ Coccydinia ■ Sacroiliac joint strain ■ Sciatica ■ Spondylolysis ■ Spondylolisthesis

16 ARM PAIN 213

■ Acromio-clavicular (AC) joint strain ■ Bursitis ■ Finger sprain ■ Fracture and dislocation ■ Frozen shoulder ■ Golfer's elbow ■ Shoulder pain ■ Tendinitis ■ Tennis elbow ■ Tenosynovitis ■ Thumb pain ■ Wrist sprain

17 LEG PAIN 226

■ Ankle sprain ■ Anterior thigh pain ■ Calf pain ■ Foot sprain ■ Groin pain ■ Hip and buttock pain ■ Knee pain ■ Metatarsalgia ■ Posterior thigh pain ■ Shin pain ■ Sprain

18 FINDING YOUR MANUAL PRACTITIONER 239

■ Recommendation ■ The telephone book ■ Making a phone call ■ Approach treatment sceptically ■ Assess the rate of progress ■ Resources

GLOSSARY 245

INDEX 246

INTRODUCTION

Every one of us, myself included, suffers some joint and muscular discomfort from time to time. If the trouble won't go away or keeps coming back it won't be long before you are receiving advice from your friends, relations and work colleagues about how they cured exactly the same problem. With great enthusiasm they will explain how their own personal magician, who has the most marvellous hands, can fix almost anything in the blink of an eye and with just the flick of a wrist. They are describing manual therapy, one of the most popular and sought out treatments for everyday aches and pains.

Manual therapy is the general term used to describe a family of therapies that involve the use of the hands to treat problems, mainly affecting the muscles and joints. These therapies are wide ranging and include massage, chiropractic, manual physiotherapy, osteopathy and manual medicine. Like dentistry, podiatry and optometry, the manual therapies complement and add to the scope of mainstream medicine.

A manual approach can be the ideal way to treat painful back and neck problems due to physical strain. It also works well on disorders that affect the arms and legs. Moreover, manual therapy can help some conditions that don't appear to have suffered from strain. Excellent results can be achieved with tension-type headaches, migraine, certain visual disturbances, and even some problems affecting the digestive and respiratory systems.

It is especially pleasing to me that manual therapy is able to give relief and hope to those suffering painful, morale-sapping conditions that have previously resisted the best medical treatment available. Sometimes the problem cannot be treated in any other way. In most cases, people seem to be very satisfied with their treatment.

The purpose of this book

While the community is becoming increasingly accepting of manual therapy, many still don't realise its full potential. Manual therapy is seen to complement mainstream medical treatment, but it still doesn't quite have the full approval of orthodox medicine. It's becoming more mainstream, but it still gets confused with less acceptable alternatives. *Pain Relief* has been written to help demystify manual therapy for those who are curious about what it is and how it could help them.

Most people have never experienced any form of manual therapy, although many will have suffered from discomfort in the muscles and joints from time to time. These problems may be a worry to you now and again, or they may be disturbing in a more troublesome way. You may have tried other treatment without results and want to find out more about your problem and what else might help. *Pain Relief* will give you guidance in deciding whether manual therapy is appropriate for you or not.

Others will have experienced manual therapy from a masseur, chiropractor, osteopath, physiotherapist or medical practitioner at one time or another. They often have questions about this treatment method. Moreover, the patient's family and friends might be curious and ask: 'What's going on, and what does the treatment involve?' This book will provide you with some answers.

More and more, medical practitioners are considering using a manual therapy approach for their patients. The British Medical Association, in its book *Complementary Medicine, New Approaches to Good Practice*, sees it as essential that doctors should know more about other treatments so that they can advise their patients about the most appropriate treatment available. *Pain Relief* gives health professionals an overview of the various manual methods.

I've tried to avoid mumbo jumbo and specialised jargon when explaining how manual therapy works and what manual practitioners really do. Any information is, of course, based on established and accepted scientific knowledge. If the information is theoretical or best guess, I will try to make that clear.

I have divided the book into two parts. Part One, 'What is Manual Therapy and How Can It Help?' explains manual therapy and explores the basic ideas, how it works, how problems are diagnosed, types of treatment and their effects, its history and the different sub-disciplines. It will give you insights into the commonly asked questions: 'Have I put something out?', 'Where does the crack come from?', 'Is manipulation dangerous?', 'What's the difference between the different branches of manual therapy?', and 'Do I have to keep going back?'

Part Two, 'A Guide to Symptoms and What They Might Mean', describes 60 of the most common problems that manual therapists treat and that respond positively to manual therapy. Each has its own specific causes and well-defined forms of treatment, and I will discuss the role of manual therapy in each case. Finally, there are suggestions on how you can go about finding your own good manual practitioner.

Over the years, the manual professions have tended to be protective about their methods and codes of practice. Some of my colleagues are quite adamant that each discipline is completely separate to and different from the other. They may think that I have been unfaithful to my profession for bringing the manual therapies together under one banner. However, the general public, other healthcare professions and government bodies do not necessarily see it that way; it's one reason why we are so often asked, 'How are we different?'

In reality, the manual therapies are much better understood as a group rather than separately. We all use our hands to treat the same problems, so it is unlikely that each profession is doing anything dramatically different. It is clear that these professions have a lot in common. As the various practitioners become better trained and more competent and responsible, and as the research evidence unfolds, it is inevitable that the various disciplines will converge. Practitioners can sometimes be so busy promoting their own approach that they fail to realise just how similar their methods already are to those of their manual practitioner colleagues.

The basic techniques

Manual therapy is known as such because we use our hands. We 'palpate' — that is, feel the tissues — to assess their shape, texture and response to movement. It is a kind of tactile detective process, used to sense the clues that will help diagnose the problem.

We then use our hands to administer therapeutic forces. We apply physical pressure and move parts of the body, paying attention to muscles, ligaments, fascia, joints and bones. We use kneading, stroking and friction techniques with various degrees of pressure — all familiar massage techniques. We can also move the joints in various ways, and apply rhythmic rocking to stretch and loosen the tissues that connect the bones. Sometimes we manipulate and apply a precise controlled impulse to help free up a specific joint.

A variety of other physical techniques may be added. These can include cold, heat, electrical stimulation, braces, traction and exercises to help restore the body to physical health.

Good manual therapy is a highly skilled art and does not come easily. Good manual practitioners have aptitude and take years to develop their 'touch'. They share a sensitivity commonly seen in creative and artistic occupations such as art and dance.

Manual therapy does much more than just make a person physically comfortable. Those who have experienced the total relaxation, physical pleasure and exhilaration that occurs after manual therapy, know well the dramatic improvement that they also feel in their disposition. It's not unusual for a client to smile sheepishly and say: 'I must be getting better, my partner says I'm much more bearable to live with!' Restoration of comfort and ease of movement mean that aggression, negativity and depression are replaced by calm, clear and optimistic thinking.

The question of safety

Those who are unfamiliar with manual therapy may consider some of the practices to be strange, even alarming. We think of our backs as fragile, and if we are placed in awkward positions we can feel vulnerable. Some of the manual techniques can involve a momentary impulse just at the point when we're becoming relaxed. There may be a sharp cracking noise that can be unsettling.

I should stress from the start that the techniques used by manual therapists emphasise safety and a gentle approach, and you should feel reassured that the forces involved are precisely controlled and actually quite minor. The Royal College of General Practitioners in their *Clinical Guidelines for the Management of Acute Low Back Pain*, 1996, says: 'The risks of manual therapy are very low in skilled hands'. We manual practitioners are particularly aware of the concerns people have.

While adverse effects arising from manual therapy occasionally do occur, they are much less frequent than commonly supposed. One guide to the risks, and a better indication than rumour and gossip, is the level of premiums manual practitioners pay for professional malpractice insurance — this protects the public against mistakes and negligence. A manual practitioner pays less than 20 per cent of the amount paid by a general medical practitioner for the same level of cover. This is a remarkable difference considering the way manual therapy has been painted in the past by the medical profession.

Most manual practitioners are well aware of their limitations. The techniques have now been in use for over a century and over that time practitioners have gradually learnt to restrict their techniques to a narrow but common range of complaints. They are trained to assess every patient individually, to distinguish between manual and non-manual disorders, and to refer the latter for medical assessment and treatment.

PART ONE
WHAT IS MANUAL THERAPY AND HOW CAN IT HELP?

CHAPTER ONE

BODY MECHANICS

■ The basic insight ■ How mechanical disorders develop ■ How manual therapy works ■ Where does the pain come from? ■ The pain—spasm—pain cycle ■ Collagen, the body's glue ■ Predisposing conditions ■ Advantages of manual therapy

Historically, medical thinking and teaching have tended to focus on organ systems. The circulation, heart, respiration, digestion, reproduction and the endocrine systems all have their own unique disease processes and injuries. Orthodox medicine has regarded the body's musculoskeletal framework as more secondary, a 'coat-hanger' on which the organs are hung.

Manual practitioners see the human body in a different way. We don't live our lives to circulate blood, breathe, digest, filtrate or secrete. Instead we run, walk, talk, laugh, write, drive, work and play. Everything we think, do, create and achieve in life is expressed through physical activity. It is extraordinary to think that life as we know it is only seen through the movements of the human body.

Professor Irvine Korr, physiologist, has called our musculoskeletal system the 'primary machinery of life'. All other organs are, in a way, secondary, because their job is to transport, nourish, repair, service and generally maintain this primary machinery through which we express and enjoy our lives. To work, the musculoskeletal system must be served by the circulatory, respiratory, digestive, genitourinary and endocrine systems; they are the support systems to the primary machinery. We manual practitioners are concerned with understanding the musculoskeletal primary machinery, why it sometimes fails and how we can help it to recover.

The basic insight

Manual therapy is based on a fundamental idea. We apply our manual techniques to a small family of tissues called the 'soft tissues' in order to treat the large number of conditions that we see.

The soft tissues are the tissues that connect the bones, or 'hard tissues'. There are only five types of soft tissue: muscle, ligament, joint capsule, fascia and, in the spine, disc. The soft tissues give joints flexibility and the power to move.

In manual therapy, treatment is directed towards the soft tissues and has little to do with bones. We feel for abnormalities in the soft tissues, apply treatment to the soft tissues and detect improvement within the soft tissues. This central point — that manual therapy is all about the soft tissues and not the bones — is not widely understood by the public and, to some extent, is insufficiently expressed by manual practitioners.

'Mechanical disorder' refers to all the conditions we manual practitioners treat, and is a term used throughout this book. Mechanical disorder is a general term like psychiatric disorder, orthopaedic condition or dental problem. Mechanical disorders are seen and felt as conditions where there is altered soft tissue texture and joint mobility, with or without underlying disease. They are often provoked and aggravated by physical overload, and include prolapsed disc, tendinitis, osteoarthritis, joint strain, and a host of problems that can affect every aspect of our daily lives.

Manual therapy can also help some mechanical problems

that cause symptoms affecting the abdomen and chest. These account for only a small part of our caseload, but the relief can be profound.

Manual therapy can also put right mechanical disorders causing discomfort that arise not from physical strain but from emotional stress and fatigue.

> Jade, a 37-year-old mother, works in a demanding job managing a medical product distributorship. Jade is already working close to her limit, so she decides it s time to make life simpler and change her job. At the same time as she is preparing a new personal profile and looking for a job, Jade s elderly mother has a fall and needs to be regularly visited at home. The extra pressures cause Jade s previously troublesome neck aches, shoulder aches and headaches to reappear. Jade seeks out a manual therapist who is able to give considerable relief for her headaches and neck pain. This allows her to continue with the extra demands placed on her without the physical discomfort.

How mechanical disorders develop

The capacity of our bodies to withstand mechanical loads without harm depends on how much stress is imposed and whether the tissues can stand the strain. The back of a strong, healthy adult male might be strained by moving too much heavy furniture, whereas a neck previously damaged by a whiplash injury might easily seize up due to the person simply looking over their shoulder. You can have too much force or too little strength. They are opposite sides of the same coin.

Excessive force occurs through all sorts of twists, strains, impacts and falls. It can be produced by any kind of physical activity, from computer work to cleaning, assembly work to sport. Muscles and tendons can be painfully sprained, ligaments can suffer partial tears, joints can undergo acute strain and discs can become prolapsed. Too much force might cause a calf muscle to tear as you lunge for a tennis ball, a disc prolapse can develop as you stoop over to change a car tyre, or you might strain your upper back through doing some unaccustomed and prolonged keyboarding.

Too little strength means that a body part has a reduced ability to withstand physical strain. An old injury with scar tissue, general wear and tear, joint disease, joints suffering through lack of use, or mental stress can all change the soft tissues, leaving them tense, hardened, fibrous and inelastic. In this state they are more susceptible to overload and damage. Activities such as reaching, turning and bending, walking, driving, deskwork and jogging, which are often taken for granted, may be enough to injure and cause symptoms.

> Jan has been a nurse for 30 years. Twenty-five years ago she injured her back helping to lift an unconscious patient. This occurred well before occupational regulations about maximum lifting loads were taken seriously. At the time, Jan had six weeks off work but the injury never really recovered, despite the fact that she did have some treatment. Her back grumbled and hurt in the same old spot whenever she did too much,

both at work and around the home and garden. She sought help from practitioners from time to time, but the problem never seemed to resolve itself.

On the occasion that Jan came to see me she had been doing her normal nursing duties, but on reaching for an instrument had felt an acute stab of pain in the area of her old injury.

I frequently see patients with similar stories of old injuries that never fully recovered at the time, that constantly grumble, and flare up when the sufferer makes a trivial movement. These types of problems are highly suited to manual therapy.

How manual therapy works

The manual professions agree on three fundamental points. Firstly, when we are looking for a mechanical problem, we try to find an abnormality in the texture of the soft tissues that connect the bones. We feel for tissues that are inflamed and swollen, tense and shortened, thickened and hard. Palpation can be likened to finding the lumps in a cake-mix of flour and butter. We find the lumps and gently smooth them out.

Secondly, we try to gently move and feel for joints that are stiff and restricted in range. This can give us information about the deeper soft tissues joining two bones. These are less accessible and often cannot be felt directly. Although spinal movements are small, they are not that hard to feel. With the eyes closed, anyone can tell the difference between a live twig and a dead one. The live twig is springy and has give; the dead one is rigid and stiff. Feeling for a stiff spinal joint is very similar.

Thirdly, to help confirm the exact problem spot, we might ask the patient if he or she experiences tenderness when the suspect site is carefully probed, and whether the probing reproduces the discomfort of the problem.

By checking for these three key features — the texture of the soft tissues, the mobility of the joints and whether the symptoms of tenderness can be reproduced — manual practitioners will be able to confirm the presence or absence of a mechanical disorder. The jury is still out on other tests, such as bony position, skin temperature and skin sweatness. Individual practitioners and professions might use them but they do not have the support of all manual practitioners.

Another key point, and the goal of manual therapy, is that we try to reverse our palpation findings and restore pliant soft tissues and mobile joints. In treatment we gently relax muscles, soften ligaments and loosen the joints. Using our various treatment techniques, we gradually tip the balance from shortening, thickening and stiffening towards relaxation, suppleness and motion.

> Bob, a strapping 32-year-old surfer, was doing some major work in the garden, clearing his fence line before the fencing contractor was due to erect a new fence. Towards the end of the afternoon, as he was reaching for a spade, he was immobilised by a sharp pain in his back, near his right shoulder blade. The pain was made worse when he tried to take a big breath or twisted his body. When I examined him at the practice there was visible bulging of his back muscles near his right shoulder blade. I could feel that the muscle was hard when I gently palpated it; it reacted to pressure by contracting and making Bob flinch. When I examined movement by lightly pushing on each vertebra, there was a localised restriction between two thoracic vertebrae. Bob readily confirmed I was right on the spot . All the symptoms and signs indicated a strain of a segment at this level of Bob s back.

In Bob's case, the hard muscle spasm was initially treated with a heat pack, followed by several minutes of ultrasound. The muscle felt softer as the overlying spasm lessened, but the deeper muscle was still delicate and felt 'soggy' and congested to the touch. A few minutes of slow, gentle massage allowed me to further relax muscle tension and reduce congestion. At this point I was aware that there was better movement with some 'give' between the two vertebrae — the deeper muscles were starting to let go. It was time to try loosening the joint with small oscillations of pressure applied to the vertebra, called mobilisation. As Bob became more comfortable during the session it was clear that the problem would benefit from gentle manipulation. This added a further improvement in the range of motion and reduction in pain. Each step of Bob's treatment built on the one before to help restore the texture of the muscles and joint flexibility. Bob left the practice moving and breathing a lot more comfortably than when he had arrived. He was happy to be over the worst.

At a more fundamental level, manual therapy achieves a great deal more than just restoring supple soft tissues and mobile joints. Accomplishing these goals has a profound effect on fluid movement. Fluid flows, or the lack of them, are of great importance for the health of all living tissues. Our various manual procedures help flush out and cleanse the vessels, the fluid-filled spaces between the cells, and the contents of the cells themselves. Movement reduces sluggish fluid exchange and tissue barriers made impermeable by scar tissue, inflammation and swelling. Fluid flows deliver oxygen, nutrients and vital chemicals to the body and remove carbon dioxide, inflammatory products and all kinds of toxic wastes. Fluid movement washes away irritation and switches off the pain sensors. Fluid circulation renews the environment around and within cells and optimises healing.

These concepts of movement and fluid exchange are now widely accepted in medicine. Patients who have been hospitalised through injury, illness or operation are encouraged to become active and return home as soon as practicable. It's not only done to free up hospital beds! A knee replacement patient will wake to the whirr of a continuous passive motion machine which gently bends and straightens the knee. Early activity speeds up healing, reduces complications and lowers costs.

Based on worldwide medical evidence, the same ideas have revolutionised thinking about back care. Except in the acute stage, it has been observed that those who cope best with bad backs are the people who stay active and remain mobile. Those who lie about and avoid activity suffer the most. They have pain for longer, they have more time off work and they can become disabled.

Television advertising by government agencies and industrial workers compensation organisations reinforces this thinking. They promote the idea of 'Be active to be healthy', emphasising exercise, sport and a return to work instead of a lazy couch-potato lifestyle of immobility and rest. It's no surprise to manual practitioners that movement has become so important to health and modern living. As millions of people like Bob will testify, mobility has always been our goal.

Where does the pain come from?

Everybody experiences musculoskeletal pain at some stage in their life. It is by far the most common reason to seek help from a manual practitioner. Pain is a central survival mechanism for all animals, from one-celled organisms to complex human beings. Pain sends a dominant and compelling message. We stop, review the situation, rest, seek help and sometimes learn to avoid the situation in the future.

Although not always true, it is generally recognised that pain is a signal that some part of the body has been damaged. In the main, the intensity of pain is proportional to the severity of the injury. If the skin is pinched it produces a mild pain; when a hammer hits a finger the pain can be excruciating.

A mechanical disorder stimulates pain nerves in five ways. Immediately a tissue is injured, some of the delicate network of pain-sensing fibres passing through the injured tissue are directly affected and send off a burst of impulses to the brain. This is when we say 'ouch!' At the same time, the injury ruptures cell walls, causing them to spill their contents. These cell chemicals are irritants that stimulate the pain nerve endings.

Over the following hours, inflammation, the reaction of tissues to injury, develops to repair the damage. During this process, chemicals with weird and wonderful names, such as prostaglandin, 5-hydroxytryptamine and bradykinin, are released. These substances stimulate the pain sensors. Then, if the inflammation produces sufficient swelling, the fine nerve fibres in the region can become stretched, adding to the pain. This is when a strained ankle becomes swollen and aching.

The stimulation of the pain receptors, in turn, leads to muscle spasm. This is an involuntary reflex and a universal response to pain. The contraction serves to splint the region and protect it from further harm. Every painful musculoskeletal disorder leads to this line of defence. Unfortunately, muscle spasm itself is painful.

The pain-spasm-pain cycle

For the muscles to contract they must have energy. This comes from oxygen and glucose. If the contracting muscle does not receive enough oxygen we experience pain, known as ischaemic pain.

Ischaemic pain is a common experience to most people. Swimmer's cramp is ascribed to a reduced blood flow and therefore oxygen to the leg muscles when blood is diverted to a full stomach. Now you know why your mother told you not to swim for an hour after eating lunch! Olympic runners and gym junkies who 'pump iron' feel ischaemic pain when their muscles work flat out. Angina is pain in the chest due to clogged up coronary arteries and a shortage of oxygen to the heart muscle. Claudication is pain in one or both legs when walking, due to narrowed or blocked leg arteries. Sufferers typically have to stop walking and take a short rest to allow sufficient blood flow to be restored before they can resume walking. The cause of cramps at night is not fully understood; however, it is known that insufficient blood flow to the involved muscle is part of the process.

In the mechanical problems seen by manual practitioners, muscles in spasm require much more oxygen than those at rest. At the same time, the sustained contraction squeezes off and reduces the flow of blood within the muscle. Together, the increased demand for oxygen and insufficient supply causes ischaemic pain.

In addition, muscle spasm produces large amounts of waste chemicals. These can overload the disposal system, which normally works like a pump as the muscle alternately tenses and relaxes. These excess waste products, such as lactic acid, are irritants that contribute to pain.

Painful reflex spasm is circular and self-sustaining, and a problem that manual practitioners are always sorting out. We call it the pain–spasm–pain cycle. Pain causes muscle spasm, which in turn causes more pain. Pain from muscle spasm is frequently the greatest source of discomfort and can even exceed the pain of the original injury. The significance of muscular pain in mechanical disorders cannot be overstated. A major part of manual therapy is designed to interrupt and break the cycle of pain–spasm–pain.

When we speak of spasm, we are generally referring to

hypertonia; this is the correct term and it is the more common response to a mechanical disorder. Hypertonia is a sustained but less intense contraction than spasm. It corresponds with the lower levels of pain encountered in mechanical disorders compared with more severe traumas such as dislocation and fracture.

> When Con strained the shoulder of his throwing arm during a water polo match he experienced pain and protective muscle hypertonia. Despite the hypertonia, Con was still able to gently use the shoulder to shower, dry and dress himself before making arrangements to have it looked at later in the day. In contrast, when he dislocated the same shoulder the following year, again while playing water polo, the agonising muscle spasm prevented any sort of shoulder movement at all. The spasm was so intense that a general anaesthetic was needed to relax the shoulder muscles before the shoulder could be put back into place.

Collagen, the body's glue

Collagen is an extraordinary substance, a crucial and plentiful protein that cements and holds the body together. If all the body cells were removed, collagen alone would preserve the human form in every last detail. Collagen and muscle are the two types of tissue that manual practitioners treat.

Collagen is to animals what cellulose is to plants — fundamental to the strength of living tissue. Collagen strengthens every single structure from the external skin to the core of the bones. It is an incredibly tough molecule, requiring a load in excess of 10 000 times its own weight to stretch it. Bonded together, collagen is stronger than steel wire; without it the body would be pulled to shreds.

The long white collagen fibres are not living cells but

protein chains secreted through the walls of cells called fibroblasts. They respond to local conditions in each area to form fibres that are arranged in many different ways.

Collagen is not well known to most people, apart from those familiar with cosmetics, because it occurs in various guises. It is known by a profusion of names, such as fascia, tendon, ligament and joint capsule. It makes up the toughness of skin, is found in the strong filmy sacks that bag the muscles and organs, forms a dense mesh throughout bones and cartilage, as well as the cord-like tendons, the padded discs of the spine, the fibrous ligaments linking bones, and even the glassy cornea of the eye.

The process of acute strain and chronic injury involves the production and maturation of a form of collagen called 'scar tissue'. As the body repairs an injury, scar tissue forms; it is a natural part of the healing process. Every time the skin is broken we see scar tissue. A scar can remain visible for the rest of a person's life.

Unfortunately, scar tissue quite often overdoes its function, creating its own problems by producing excessive collagen deposits with unwanted bonding between its fibres. This overproduction of collagen is also called scar tissue. So confusingly, scar tissue can be both normal and healthy or abnormal and troublesome. In this book we are mainly interested in the bothersome variety.

The longer a tissue takes to heal, the greater the chances of bothersome scar tissue. Generally, more severe injuries take longer to heal and are therefore more likely to produce too much scar tissue. However, a mild injury can also produce excess scar tissue if physical stress is placed on the injured area before it has achieved full strength.

> Graham mildly sprained his ankle early on in the basketball season. It was not enough to stop him from training or playing, and he didn t want to miss out on the fun or let his team down, but each time he trained or played his ankle would ache for a

day or so afterwards. Each time Graham went on court he was mildly re-injuring his ankle and building up scar tissue. By the end of the basketball season, Graham had well-established scar tissue. The ankle felt stiff whenever he pointed his foot down or pulled his toes back. It felt weak and vulnerable when he changed direction or ran on rough surfaces like grass. Graham never did anything about it, thinking that in time it would get better. It was still apparent, to some extent, five years later when he came to see me about a back complaint and I asked whether there were any other problem areas. Fortunately, longstanding stiffness problems like this respond quickly and easily to manual therapy; it was sorted out at the same time as his back.

Scar tissue is a major factor in the stiffening, shortening and thickening of mechanical disorders. Excess and poorly formed collagen frequently leaves limited movement, which predisposes future damage.

Collagen, in its different forms, and muscle are the keys to manual therapy. Collagen and muscle mediate between the physical forces of manual therapy and health in the musculoskeletal system.

For many women, collagen is a household name in cosmetics and beauty care, but few know exactly what it means. Usually purified from cowhide, collagen plays two separate roles in cosmetics. When used in a skin cream, collagen is a moisturiser that holds onto water and helps to prevent dry and flaky skin. When used to fill out under wrinkles and sagging skin, injected collagen provides a natural padding. A collagen molecule is large and the only way collagen can be placed under the skin is by injection. Doctors inject it to cushion and plump up under crows' feet under the eyes, character lines and worry furrows, and to increase the size and contour of the lips. Unfortunately these measures are only temporary. They last about 18 months as the collagen gradually breaks down and disappears.

Predisposing conditions

While you would think most injuries occur when people are doing something strenuous or physically stressful, you would be surprised how often people seem to hurt themselves doing common everyday activities. Manual practitioners often hear: 'I just leant over and felt something give', 'I turned and felt a spasm', 'I stretched and became stuck' or 'It came on for no reason'.

Frequently, it appears to our palpating fingers that the soft tissues were already in unsound condition before the latest symptoms were felt. Soft tissues feel thicker, harder and more fibrous, and joints have a reduced range of motion. Time and again we find evidence of a more longstanding underlying condition. The predisposing condition seems to diminish the soft tissue's ability to accept mechanical loads and stress. It can include scar tissue from previous injury, disease, disuse, aging, fatigue, emotional stress and the repetitive strains of daily living.

Predisposing conditions not only lead to reduced physical capacity and therefore ease of injury but also seem to reduce the capacity for healing, making recovery slower.

Previous injury

Much of the lingering trouble after injury involves collagen. Scar tissue after injury or operation is newly laid collagen. 'Fibrosis' is a denser production of collagen in response to injury. It can be felt months or years later as firm thickenings, tough stringy bands or fibrous lumps under the skin. 'Adhesions' are collagen strands that bind normally unconnected structures together, preventing them from slipping past one another.

Excessive and troublesome scar tissue can interfere with the restoration of free movement. Undue scar tissue makes soft tissues slightly shorter, less pliant and fibrous in texture. In this state the tissues are susceptible to damage so that even the normal activities of daily living are sufficient to exceed their capacity.

Manual therapy can counter scar tissue by reducing unwanted 'cross-links' gluing the strands of collagen together, increasing the distance between fibres, and by promoting absorption of immature filaments. Restoration of circulation, fluid exchange and healthy chemical balance seems to halt and reverse excessive collagen production and help dissolve bonds between its fibres.

> Marion, aged 52, had a long history of recurring lower back pain and sciatica. On the occasion that she came to see me she had been experiencing daily lower back pain since a golfing holiday 12 months earlier. The pain radiated out to the back of her thigh, calf and heel. There was a constant tight, tingling sensation in the calf and heel, and when the back of the heel was tapped with a patella hammer, she had lost the reflex ankle jerk, indicating a pinched nerve. It sounded suspiciously like another prolapsed disc. Curiously, the only way Marion could ease her leg was to lie on her front with her knee bent. On further questioning, Marion said that her back and thigh did improve from time to time, but the calf did not. Whenever she

walked too far everything was stirred up again. Also, she thought the ankle reflex might have been like that since the start of her troubles years ago, because it was absent every time her doctor had tested it.

Marion then described how she had badly torn her calf muscle on the tennis court some years ago; this was the reason she had given up tennis and started playing golf. Here was something worth checking out. It was immediately obvious that there was a large, fibrous knot of scar tissue in the middle of her calf. I reasoned that the previous calf injury had bled extensively, leaving scar tissue and adhesions between the calf and the nerve passing through it. Normally the nerve should be unattached and able to slide slightly within the calf muscle. Maybe Marion s extra walking on her golf holiday had damaged the adhesions between the calf and nerve. It was also possible that the calf pain and limping were upsetting the lower back.

At Marion s second visit she was very excited she had had significant relief for the first time in a year. With further treatment to the scar tissue adhesions in her calf, Marion made a good recovery.

Disease

Certain diseases and syndromes (a group of symptoms and signs that occur together), such as migraine, spondylolisthesis (slippage of one vertebra on another) and Scheuermann's disease (defective growth of vertebra in children), create muscular tension, increased collagen, stiff movements and reduced range.

Without curing the underlying condition, manual therapists can relax and loosen the tight soft tissues that allow symptoms to arise. If left untreated, the soft tissue changes become entrenched and cause problems later on. We can alleviate both the present painful symptoms and the potential for future trouble.

> For twenty years, Cathy, aged 33, suffered intermittently from debilitating attacks of migraine. Recently, they became more frequent and seemed to be triggered by her demanding new job as a real estate consultant. Manual therapy is often helpful for people with migraine, even though the condition is a genetic disorder. Every time Cathy had a migraine, the muscles at the top of her neck would also tighten. Gradually the muscles failed to relax fully between episodes and the upper neck joints became increasingly stiff. The mechanical changes had added another trigger to the migraine.

By treating the tense muscles and stiff joints, manual therapy has allowed Cathy to obtain an immediate reduction in the frequency and severity of her migraines. She has also been able to reduce her medication considerably and will have fewer attacks in the future. Manual therapy can remove the mechanical trigger for Cathy's headaches, even though it cannot change her genetic disposition.

Adaptive stiffness

Sustained immobilisation can lead to adaptive stiffness. Put a knee or arm joint in plaster of Paris for six weeks and it can take six months for it to recover. Less dramatically, sustained muscle spasm, hypertonia, a brace, or lack of use can limit movement and result in adaptive stiffness. Again, the culprit is collagen, as it develops 'cross-links' between its fibres, hindering mobility. Stiffer tissues are always more easily injured than healthy flexible ones. However, they can also affect things in other ways.

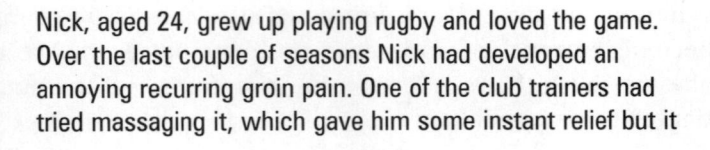

> Nick, aged 24, grew up playing rugby and loved the game. Over the last couple of seasons Nick had developed an annoying recurring groin pain. One of the club trainers had tried massaging it, which gave him some instant relief but it

continued to nag him. The club doctor then checked for medical problems affecting the kidney and for any signs of a hernia. He decided Nick s troubles were mechanical and that some physiotherapy was needed. Nick was given groin, hamstring and back stretching exercises, and ultrasound, but this wasn t very successful either.

As an ex-player and an avid fan myself, I see a lot of rugby players. Nick came to me about his problem and told me how he was increasingly sore after each training session and often woke in the morning with groin pain, only to find it eased after a hot shower and a little moving about. I looked at his leg, hip and groin and could find nothing there, so I switched my attention to his back. Nick had the typical build of a rugby forward squat with thickset muscles. Rugby had further developed his hip and back muscles.

I noticed as he bent in the various directions that Nick s lower back hardly moved at all, whereas there was exaggerated movement slightly further up, at the junction of his thoracic and lumbar spine. Nick s highly developed lower back muscles were so thick and strong that they were splinting and protecting the lower back like a corset. His lower back had adaptive stiffness, which caused overloading stresses further up. It was the thoraco-lumbar spine that was giving Nick referred pain to the groin.

A lot of rugby players, weight trainers and athletes have this form of adaptive stiffness, where muscle development protects and splints one region but causes overload in another. Treatment is simple — relax and loosen the adaptive stiffness. In Nick's case, improved mobility down below reduced the stresses further up, removing the pain referred to his groin.

Aging

As the body ages, the collagen fibres holding us together gradually mature. They tend to thicken, dry out, pack together more closely and increase their bonding, particularly where they receive the greatest pressure or strain. Aged and arthritic joints gradually become stiff in movement, limited in range and distorted in shape. There is no way of preventing the natural, gradual drying and stiffening of aging collagen.

Degenerative changes mostly proceed silently and, mercifully, without pain or inflammation. But the margin between an arthritic but painless and functioning joint and a painfully disabled joint becomes narrowed. Small strains or increases in physical activity can create pain and disability, apparently out of proportion to the cause.

> Barb, at only 53, had significant degeneration in the joint at the base of her big toe. With no knowledge of any previous injury, she found the joint was often painful, swollen and intolerant of fashionable shoes. A round of her beloved game of golf was always uncomfortable. X-rays demonstrated marked joint wear with near total loss of the normal layers of cartilage between the two bones. Over the past 10 years Barb has seen me from time to time to ease the discomfort and improve her walking distance. So far, an operation has been avoided, but in due course it will become inevitable. In the meantime, Barb finds that manual therapy keeps her problem under control.

Fatigue and emotional stress

Stress is a major determinant of health; some think it is the overriding cause of ill health. Its effects are often felt in the musculoskeletal system. Fatigue, emotional stress and unresolved conflict all increase muscular tension and can directly lead to pain, add pain to existing discomfort or aggravate an old problem. The head, neck and shoulders are frequently involved.

At some stage of our lives, almost all of us experience emotional tension that causes or exacerbates physical discomfort. Remember those exams, perhaps the difficult teenage years, stressful times at work, money troubles, the pain of selling and moving house or trying to come to terms with a relationship breakdown. Often the outcomes are neck pain, headaches and an unresolved situation. The pain often seems to pick on areas that have given trouble before. While you may be unable to resolve your life situation immediately, there are numerous ways of handling the emotional and physical discomfort. One of the most useful and immediate is massage or other forms of manual therapy; others could include walking the dog, taking up some active exercise such as swimming or gym workouts, taking medication or seeking out some counselling.

Not surprisingly, any or all of the predisposing conditions (previous injury, disease, adaptive stiffness, aging, fatigue and emotional problems) can occur together and in any proportion to make mechanical problems more complex, entrenched and unresponsive to treatment.

Manual therapy is unequalled in its ability to seek out tense and hardened soft tissues that oppose movement and vital fluid exchange. Our highly skilled and focused treatment techniques can dramatically shift the body's tolerance of physical demands.

While the various predisposing conditions are frequent factors in the development, recurrence and persistence of mechanical disorders, I should emphasise that physical overload and damage often occurs without any underlying problem to weaken the tissues. Injuring strong and healthy tissues always requires greater or more prolonged physical stress.

Advantages of manual therapy

'It works' may be good enough for some of our clients who obtain relief from manual therapy. But others ask, 'What is it that makes manual therapy so effective compared with other treatments I have tried?' Manual therapy has a number of important advantages that both patients and practitioners find very satisfying and real.

For a start, assessment is based on touching the problem. It is this diagnostic skill which really distinguishes manual therapy. We manual practitioners develop a highly refined sense of touch. A manual practitioner can discover, often without help, the source of a problem and confirm that its characteristics match the patient's history and symptoms. At the same time, the patient senses that their problem is thoroughly explored and identified in a very real way. The diagnostic process of touching the problem simply feels right.

In treatment, our therapeutic techniques can be precisely localised to any individual joint. Clearly, it would be unhelpful to manipulate the wrist or the shoulder if it was the elbow at fault. The same applies to treating the first or third joint in the neck instead of a problem in between. It simply requires greater knowledge, training and skill to accomplish it.

Tran, a computer programmer, came to see me about a recurring, persistent pain he was experiencing between his shoulder blades. He had joined a gym in an effort to ease the pain and was also taking anti-inflammatory tablets. Despite some ease, neither exercises nor tablets completely fixed the problem. When he came to see me, a couple of joints between his shoulder blades were stiff and painful and clearly the source of his trouble. Tran was given three treatments of massage, mobilisation and manipulation to relax the muscles and loosen the problem joints. It gave him immediate benefit with full and sustained recovery.

This demonstrates the difference between non-specific (exercise and paracetamol) and well-focused treatment (manual therapy). Our capacity to focus on the soft tissues at fault is a major reason for the success of manual therapy.

With educated sensitivity and careful touch, manual therapists can continually monitor the response to treatment quite independently of symptoms. We can tell you exactly how far the problem has recovered. Then, we can modify therapy to suit the specific needs and progress of the problem without the patient feeling that they have been dropped onto an automated conveyer belt of treatment. There is a clear sense that each individual receives treatment appropriate to their needs.

It has been well documented that patients' attitudes to manual therapy are positive. They describe their practitioners as easy to talk to, good listeners, sincere and not condescending. People say that manual practitioners examine them more thoroughly, give them more time, and offer better explanations with greater confidence about the outcome. Patients feel that manual practitioners provide immediate help for the whole person rather than simply treating a specific illness.

Finally, as the cost of medicine soars with each advance in investigations, drugs and technology, studies have found that by comparison manual therapy is reasonably priced. Several, but not all, studies have concluded that the total cost is smaller than medical treatment for the same problem.

> Chris, aged 54, runs a busy service station. He went to see his GP about his lower back. It had given him trouble several times previously but this time it was more persistent. His doctor thought the trouble was mechanical strain and prescribed anti-inflammatory tablets. At Chris's third visit, when it was clear there was no real progress, the doctor said, Perhaps it's about time we had an X-ray. When the GP studied the X-rays, he could find nothing; apart from some early joint degeneration his X-rays were normal for his age.
>
> Although his doctor still felt that the complaint was nothing serious, Chris was more concerned, so the doctor agreed to run some blood tests, which were again negative. Next the GP recommended a course of physiotherapy. After six sessions during which time the young physio had done his best, Chris returned to his doctor still experiencing some pain.
>
> It was time for the big guns; Chris was referred to a specialist for a more comprehensive examination. He was sent for an MRI and bone scan, and handed some new sample anti-inflammatory tablets to try out. When Chris reported back for the results he was told, There's nothing to worry about. It was made clear that he was suffering the results of working hard all his life and that, as he had tried everything, at this point he would just have to learn to live with it.
>
> Chris was happy that he wasn't about to die from some dreadful illness, but he was still in pain and determined that he wasn't going to put up with it forever, despite what the doctor had said! That's when he came to our practice. After reviewing the situation, we were able to provide a different treatment approach — manual therapy. After a trial of three treatments Chris was improving. Over eight visits he became symptom-free.

> Chris could have saved himself a great deal of trouble, time, money, pain and pill-swallowing if he had received manual therapy much earlier. Every manual practitioner would smile at this sort of story; we've been hearing it for decades!

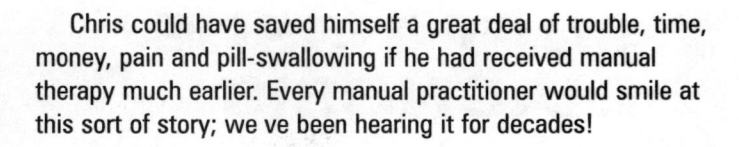

It is very satisfying when manual therapy provides such excellent and predictable outcomes. Many of the people who consult us have already 'done the rounds' and are still in pain. We often restore them to full pain-free activity and transform their lives. They recover their old energy, confidence and pleasure in life; they return to being their own true selves.

CHAPTER TWO

SOFT TISSUE DIAGNOSIS

- The soft tissues and their design
- The rest of the body framework
- Diagnosis

Before describing how manual practitioners decide exactly what is wrong, I need to explain what parts of the body we're particularly interested in and why they are so important to manual practitioners. Although the detail is complex, there are remarkably few basic building blocks. Understanding the building blocks will help you to understand what manual therapy is all about.

The bones, the soft tissues connecting them and their nerve supplies together form the neuromusculoskeletal system. We often shorten this mouthful of a term to 'musculoskeletal system', or even better, 'body frame'. This system of muscles, bones, joints and their nerves makes up approximately three-quarters of our total body weight, the muscles alone accounting for more than half the body weight.

The soft tissues and their design

The soft tissues are exactly that: soft, supple and stretchy. They connect the 'hard tissues' or bones, and give our joints flexibility and the power to move. There are five soft tissues: muscle, ligament, fascia, joint capsule and disc.

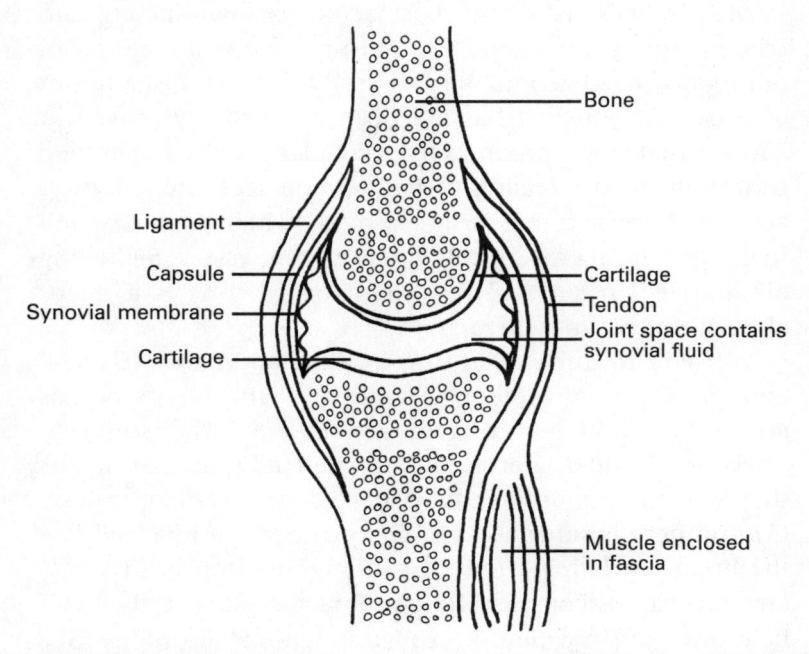

A typical joint showing muscle, tendon, ligament, bone, cartilage, fascia and capsule.

Muscle

Muscle is the most abundant tissue in the human body. There are about 300 voluntary muscles, which make up the large majority of everything under the skin. They are largely responsible for the shape and outline of our appearance. Muscles account for more than 50 per cent of the body's weight.

Muscle is composed of fibres, long slender conglomerations of cells that become shorter and thicker in response to a nerve stimulus. A number of muscle fibres are grouped together and surrounded by a thin clear membrane called fascia. Several of these groups are then organised into whole muscles coated by a thicker layer of fascia. The fascia wraps around each muscle, permeates its interior and gathers the ends into tendons.

Muscle cells have the most active cellular metabolism (chemistry) in the body. They consume the vast majority of our food and oxygen intake and produce the largest amount of waste. Although it has not been conclusively proved, it appears that waste products from cellular activity might help contribute to the feeling of fatigue you feel after physical activity. A muscle that is in spasm is switched on day and night, generating exhausting quantities of wastes. Switching off muscle tension and restoring normal tone is a major objective of manual therapy.

We tend to think of muscle in association with exercise and conscious movement, but many of the body's organs are mostly muscle — involuntary muscle. The stomach, intestines, bladder, uterus, and heart are all muscular organs that depend on muscular activity to carry out their purpose. Control here is subconscious, commanded automatically by the brain. By helping reduce excessive tension in involuntary muscle, osteopaths and chiropractors believe they can help some organ conditions called functional disorders. (See Chapter 3, Functional disorders and Chapter 14, Abdominal functional disturbance.)

In a functional problem, an organ might give troublesome symptoms but there is no pathology or evidence of tissue and cell change to indicate a medical disease. Abdominal fullness or a sense of bloating, indigestion, urinary frequency and painful periods, can be functional symptoms. Medicine tends to explain functional symptoms as indicating some sort of stress in a person's life.

Tendon

Tendon or sinew is the rounded cord joining muscle to bone. A tendon is the non-contracting part of a muscle. It is made of the same collagen fibres as the fascia that comes together at the end of a muscle.

Tendons can be quite long — up to 30 cm long in the leg. Where a tendon bends round corners, like at the wrists and ankles, a slippery tube of 'synovium' encloses it to prevent rubbing.

A tendon is so strong it is very difficult to rupture. A violent wrench is more likely to pull a fragment off the bone-tendon junction at one end, or injure its muscle-tendon junction at the other.

Inflammation of a tendon is called tendinitis — the most common injury. It is usually caused by unaccustomed, repetitive and prolonged activities, such as sporting and fitness activities when first taken up or returned to after a lengthy break, or hard playing. Gym work and training, team sports and equipment that is gripped, such as a tennis racket, can lead to tendinitis. Other seemingly innocuous tasks can also cause tendinitis if carried out for too long. These can include walking, typing, cleaning, polishing, sewing, painting and gardening.

> Brian, an active 35-year-old, proudly felled a half-dead tree in his garden using a friend s chainsaw. He wanted to use the wood in his slow combustion stove and cut the boughs into convenient sized pieces before calling it a day. The following morning, Brian knew he had worked hard his right shoulder felt painful when he lifted his arm and it took the best part of a week to settle. Two weeks later he decided it was time to remove the tree stump. It took him several hours of hard slog using a spade, axe and crowbar. This time his shoulder started to hurt as he worked, particularly when he swung the axe or levered the stump with the crowbar.
>
> Brian came to see me a week later because his shoulder hadn t settled. He had pain at the tip of the shoulder spreading down the outside of the upper arm. The pain was aggravated whenever he used the shoulder and lifted his arm sideways. On examination, it was quite clear that there was localised thickening, inflammation and tenderness over one tendon. Resisting an attempt to lift the arm sideways reproduced the pain. Brian had tendinitis.

Fascia

Fascia are fibrous sheets of collagen that wrap up, permeate and give strength, shape and support to everything in the body. An example can be seen in the tough, glossy, whitish layer on the outside of a leg of lamb. Excessive collagen in a butcher's roast is what makes tough meat chewy.

In the normal healthy state, fascia is made of relaxed wavy strands of collagen, like fibres of wool. It has the ability to slightly stretch, slide and move. When we experience physical trauma, inflammation draws in fluid and the bag of fascia becomes stretched and tight. This leads to internal pressure that hinders fluid exchange and can lead to pain.

Superficial fascia occurs immediately beneath the skin and envelops the entire body. It is particularly thick in the palms of the hands and soles of the feet, toughening and protecting them. Deep fascia wraps, lines, binds, anchors and separates into compartments every muscle, bone, nerve, vessel and organ of the body. It fixes everything firmly into place, allowing just enough mobility. Small wonder that the other name given to collagen is 'connective tissue'.

> Andy had recently retired and with his newfound freedom took up bushwalking in a serious way. He joined his local walking club and embarked on his first arduous walk. The next day, Andy was in trouble with pain in his shins. Although it eased after a day or two, Andy pushed on with his new walking passion. However, it wasn t too long before he realised he needed help. Inflammation inside the fascia bag containing his damaged shin muscle was hindering the blood flow and slowing up the natural healing response. Manual therapy enhanced the body s healing process by helping the fluids drain away, thereby allowing the inflammation to subside. As Andy grew accustomed to the long walks, his shins grew used to this type of activity.

Ligament

Ligament is a band of thick, tough and fibrous tissue across a joint that prevents the joint from moving too far. It is the restraining harness that comes into play at the extremes of movement, whereas the muscles maintain any intermediate position.

Like fascia and tendon, ligament is made of collagen and is therefore very strong. A severe ligament strain — for example, at the ankle — can be more incapacitating than a fracture because subsequent 'scar tissue' can result in a persistently stiff and complaining joint.

Double-jointed people, like gymnasts and ballet dancers, don't really have two joints; they have lax or long ligaments that allow more than the usual movement. Lax ligaments do not normally cause a problem in daily life.

Joint capsule

Enclosing and joining bone ends is the joint capsule. This is a kind of bag made, yet again, of collagen. It is a thicker, stronger layer than the filmy sheet of fascia surrounding muscle, but is not as strong as ligament. It is lined internally with a slippery synovial membrane. This membrane produces synovial fluid, the slightly greasy joint lubricant that keeps joint surfaces moist and slippery.

When you strain a joint, it's easy to think that the bones are in some way involved. But it is not possible to strain a bone. Only the fibres of the joint capsule and ligaments have been overloaded and damaged. If this happens, synovial fluid pours out of the lining membrane, filling the joint capsule to produce a swollen joint.

A doctor may diagnose a strained joint in your back. This is what some manual practitioners, and their patients, call a 'bone out of place' or misalignment. These terms really mean the joint capsule and ligaments have been overloaded and injured. They have nothing to do with the alignment of the bones.

Disc

Discs are present only in the spine and make up about a quarter of its length. They are tough, fibrous pads and join each of the vertebrae, making the whole structure flexible but strong.

A lower back (lumbar) disc has a gelatinous core, about the consistency of chewing gum. This is enclosed by a tough ring of ligament, again made of collagen. The strength of collagen makes it difficult to damage the disc, so injury is less frequent than sometimes thought.

Each disc is very firmly attached to a vertebra above and below. It is not possible literally to slip a disc out of position. The term 'slipped disc' was coined before the problem was fully understood. Slipped or, more accurately, strained or prolapsed discs, including a few of those that would otherwise lead to surgery, respond well to gentle manual therapy.

The rest of the body framework

Bone

Bones are not, of course, part of the soft tissues; they are the hard tissues. Nevertheless, they are a part of the body's mechanical framework and the soft tissues physically connect them.

They are fascinating in their own right and surprisingly active. Bones are made of a closely packed mesh of collagen strands secreted by fibroblast cells. Into this mesh calcium is deposited as hard crystals of calcium apatite. Bone is in a state of dynamic equilibrium, with calcium continually being deposited and re-absorbed, so it is constantly remoulding its shape. A bone completely changes all of its calcium every year. The structure is very strong, but also rigid — if a bone yields at all, it snaps completely.

Due to the hardness of bone, the comforting actions of manual therapy cannot soften and loosen or relax and lengthen it. Manual therapy cannot alter the shape of bone or the progress of a bone disease. And, increasingly, therapists recognise that manual therapy, and manipulation in particular, has little effect on the alignment of bones. Manual practitioners use the bones only as levers to influence the soft tissues attached to them.

While we cannot directly change the bones themselves, there is little doubt that manual therapy gives positive indirect benefits. Studies carried out on rabbits and rats show that when a joint is immobilised in plaster of Paris, degeneration is accelerated. Manual practitioners believe that by restoring movement to stiff joints they can delay cartilage wear and the development of arthritis. This can be especially important in the spine, where the spinal nerves exit past vertebral joints with narrow margins of clearance. Pressure on these nerves can be particularly troublesome and can sometimes necessitate spinal operations.

Cartilage

Where bones meet each other they are coated with smooth and slippery cartilage, or gristle. It is springy and resilient, a kind of solid lubricant, like a plastic bearing or non-stick pan.

It reduces friction and stops the bones from wearing each other away.

Cartilage, unlike other living tissues, has no blood supply. Oxygen and nutrients must therefore be diffused through the cartilage across hundreds of cells to support those that are furthest away. When injured, cartilage has the greatest difficulty in healing, and surgery may be required to remove the damaged piece.

Cartilage also has no nerve supply and therefore cannot suffer pain. The agony of a torn cartilage in the knee comes not from the cartilage itself but from damage to the tissues that tether it in place.

Nerve

A nerve is a bundle of conducting fibres that transmit electrical signals between the brain and the body. Sensory fibres conduct impulses towards the brain and motor nerves conduct impulses from the brain. Most nerves include both kinds of fibres bundled together.

Scattered throughout muscle, ligament, capsule and bone surrounds are pain nerve endings that detect damage. They are ultimately chemical sensors that respond to cell damage, waste products, inflammation and swelling. Manual practitioners have ways of turning them down or switching them off to reduce or even eliminate pain.

Nerves do not physically support the body. The muscles, ligaments and joint capsules are stretched well before a nerve feels any tension. Sliding slightly between the body tissues, they are flexible but inelastic.

It is not possible to relieve a pinched nerve by moving it away from a structure that is crushing it, such as a prolapsed disc or arthritic spur. Manual therapy helps only by reducing inflammation, compression or adherence of the tissues adjacent to the nerve.

Diagnosis

To diagnose problems of the body, we use a standardised and systematic process of assessment. Everyone is familiar with the process of a visit to the doctor. We tell the story, he or she takes a look at the problem, runs some tests and comes up with the diagnosis. Simple really!

The philosophy of diagnosis is essentially the same for any branch of healthcare. In Western culture, it is a well-established exercise in scientific deduction: collect information, form hypotheses, perform tests, eliminate options and finally, if possible, confirm one theory.

For a manual therapist, the process tells us the location, the components and the type of injury. We assess the severity and duration. We explore treatment options, work out which are most appropriate, and use the information to consult with and make recommendations to the client.

Manual practitioners tend to divide their diagnostic procedure into two parts. The medical diagnosis follows the same approach as orthodox medicine. We then go on to develop a diagnosis that is distinctive and unique to manual therapy — the mechanical diagnosis.

Medical diagnosis

For the most part, the medical diagnostic phase is used by both manual and medical practitioners, and is similar. However, during the examination we are more likely to put our hands on the patient to feel what's going on. We rely more heavily on our 'hands on' palpatory skills, whereas a medical practitioner might be more reluctant to touch.

We begin by talking to the client, to develop a picture and history of the problem. This usually narrows the field down to a handful of possible disorders. Then we give a general physical examination searching for problem spots. We look for abnormalities in areas like posture, stance, curves and walking pattern. We compare paired bony promontories. For example, the level of the hips will show whether the spine sits on a horizontal base, while elevation of one shoulder blade might indicate a scoliosis (curvature of the spine).

During this part of the assessment we are particularly interested to identify areas that we want to examine in more detail during the next 'mechanical diagnosis' phase. We observe the client in motion. We watch and feel a relevant part moving freely and against resistance, and assess its range, ease, strength, smoothness and symmetry. Pain and tenderness at this time are valuable sources of evidence.

We may integrate this information with other tests. Reflexes and skin sensation provide information about the nervous system. Heart sounds, blood pressure and pulse measure the cardiovascular function. X-rays and pathology testing of blood or urine may be needed to finally pin the problem down.

This process of detection should be sufficient to identify the condition and allow us to come to the same diagnosis as a medical practitioner. At this point, we will know whether or not the problem can be treated with manual therapy. If not, it is passed on to somebody else, most often a medical practitioner.

Mechanical diagnosis

The mechanical diagnosis provides a much more detailed map of the tissues at fault, and distinguishes manual therapy from conventional medicine. Our treatment methods are more focused and specifically tailored to the injured area than prescriptions of medicine, heat treatment, exercise and rest. It requires high-level skills in palpation and precise anatomic knowledge to identify which are the exact tissues causing the symptoms.

Manual practitioners perform their mechanical assessment in many different ways, but there are two main classes of tests that we use: soft tissue evaluation and movement testing. These are the 'non-verbal conversations' we have with our patients. A third 'test', tenderness reproducing symptoms, might help confirm the palpation findings.

In soft tissue evaluation, we use our hands to make a detailed map of the problem and its extent. Varying pressures and types of finger or hand contact probe the skin, and test the character of the underlying muscles, ligaments, joint capsules and bones. Sensitive palpation skills feel for excess muscle tension, inflammation, thickening and scar tissue. Both past and present injuries, whether low grade and grumbling or acute and intense, are there to be read in the language of the tissues.

In testing movement, we apply small degrees of motion to the joints and feel the effect of placing tension on the tissues connecting the bones. Here we feel for the range, quality, recoil and end feel. These tests enable us to build a mental picture of the deeper structures that are harder, often impossible to palpate directly.

The third test, 'tenderness reproducing symptoms', might distinguish between two nearby trouble spots and help to confirm the exact site of a problem. A manual practitioner could mistakenly decide that a nearby stiff joint is the source of trouble and treat it when it has little to do with the complaint. While this is not as disastrous as a surgeon chopping off the wrong leg, it won't necessarily help the real problem recover. To avoid this, we might gently press on a potential trouble spot and ask: 'Does this feel more tender than that?' or 'Is this the trouble spot?'

With all this information we can answer the questions that determine manual treatment. Exactly which tissues are giving rise to symptoms and why? Where should treatment begin? How much should be done and in what order? What are the techniques to use and to what degree should they be used? How many visits are likely to be needed and how long should the intervals be between them? What sort of advice, exercise or support should be given? And, most importantly, what techniques should be avoided, because of possible dangers or the presence of other disease?

> Angelica, a 48-year-old school principal, complained to her medical practitioner about lower back pain that was spreading to her right hip and the outside of the same thigh. This was not the first time it had bothered her. Before becoming principal she used to do a great deal of sport, including weight training, competitive tennis and ski-jumping. Since becoming less active Angelica had become aware that her back was giving her more trouble. This time the pain had started after a long drive home from Sydney at the end of the school holidays.
>
> Throughout the first week of term Angelica had a hectic schedule of busy days and evening meetings. All the time she was bothered by her aching back and leg. On the Friday, her first available free moment, Angelica finally saw her medical practitioner. After describing her symptoms and story the doctor took a look. He asked Angelica to bend forwards, backwards and sideways. He concluded that she had strained her lower back and prescribed anti-inflammatory tablets to be taken for two weeks. If there was no improvement in that time the doctor planned to send Angelica for X-rays. That was the extent of the medical history and examination, and all that was required in order to draw conclusions and prescribe tablets.

Although initially she felt better, over the next two weeks the pain and stiffness continued to grumble. Angelica was recommended by a school colleague to try manual therapy. After she repeated her story to me, it all became clear on examination. The two lowest joints of Angelica's back were stiff in every direction she moved; more so when she bent to the right. Also, the muscles had a hard, fibrous texture, more so on the right, that indicated longstanding origins. The spot was sensitive to touch and caused her pain in her back as well as to the outside of her thigh. By using my fingertips to explore the area I could identify the exact spot where Angelica was feeling pain. Angelica was suffering from an acute on chronic strain of the lower back.

Whereas anti-inflammatory tablets might be sufficient to reduce pain and inflammation in certain cases, they will do little to eliminate the underlying joint stiffness and address the reasons for Angelica's recurring troubles. Manual therapy can assist the medication to ease the acute pain and stiffness, and in the longer term eliminate recurrences.

CHAPTER THREE

SYMPTOMS AT A DISTANCE

- Trapped nerves ■ Referred pain
- Reflex effects ■ Functional disorders
- The role of manual therapy in symptoms at a distance ■ Mechanical disorders and medical diseases ■ Is there more to manual therapy?

Besides pain and suffering at the immediate site, mechanical problems cause a whole family of symptoms felt elsewhere in the body. These are a major and frequent part of the problems that manual practitioners successfully treat.

Not so many years ago, all remote symptoms were described as 'a trapped nerve', 'a pinched nerve' or 'pressure on a nerve'. We know now that this is far less common than previously thought. Instead, referred pain and reflex effects account for the great majority of cases. It is most important that we distinguish a trapped nerve from referred pain and reflex effects. They are often confused but they have quite different causes, treatments and rates of recovery.

When referred pain and reflex effects affect the internal organs they cause a special type of problem we call a 'functional disorder'. Here the normal behaviour or function of an organ is disturbed without any pathology (abnormal changes in tissues and cells) or physical cause within the organ.

Trapped nerves

A prolapsed disc or an arthritic bony spur might compress a nerve and interfere with the transmission of messages.

Initially there is pain, which can be burning, shooting or jabbing, occurring along a fairly narrow band in the distribution of the nerve. Then pins and needles or a fizzy sensation is felt in the distribution of the nerve. Pins and needles indicates partial pressure on the nerve. Unfortunately, pins and needles together with pain can give a horrible sensation. If the pressure increases, then numbness accompanies the pain. Reflexes tested with a patella hammer become less brisk, then disappear, and muscles supplied by the nerve become weak.

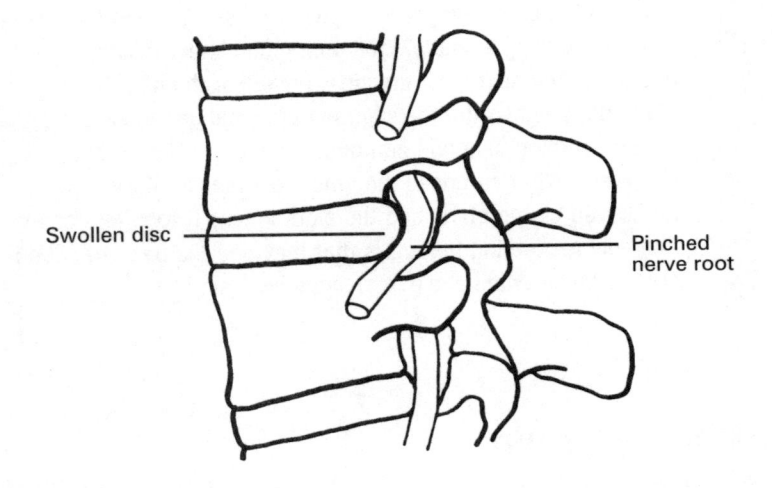

Swollen disc — Pinched nerve root

A disc and a trapped nerve

In some places, a nerve conduction study can give positive identification of a trapped nerve. In the wrist, carpal tunnel syndrome can be tested by a nerve conduction study. In this test, the nerve is given a weak electrical stimulus above the suspected point of pressure at the wrist and a measurement is made of the time it takes for the signal to pass beyond the point. A delay in the expected time taken for the stimulus to pass down into the hand indicates a pinched nerve.

Recovery from a trapped nerve is mostly uneventful but is always significantly slower than recovery from referred pain. If the pressure is sufficient and prolonged for more than a few weeks, the nerve may have to re-grow, so the numbness and weakness can take months to recover. If a nerve remains pinched for too long it can become permanently damaged. Occasionally, an operation is required to relieve pressure.

> I have suffered the misfortune of a prolapsed disc in the lower back, as I was bending over to pull out a shrub when I should have been using a spade. I felt a ping and knew things were not good. The next day I couldn t move. For the next ten days I lay on my right side, the slightest provocation increasing the intense burning pain and numbness in the front of my thigh and knee. What surprised me was the intensity of the pain, unrelieved by morphine and the eight weeks it took to recover. The only redeeming feature is that they say the best practitioners are those who have experienced illness!

Referred pain

Referred pain is a common and well-recognised medical phenomenon where the nervous system plays inconvenient tricks on the patient and diagnostician. For example, a tension headache is due to muscles under the base of the skull contracting. This causes pain, referred over the head, sometimes as far as the eyes and face. Monthly period pain can refer pain from the womb to the lower back and upper thighs. Referred pain feels diffuse and hard to localise, but it is without the tingling, numbness, altered reflexes or muscle weakness that signifies a trapped nerve.

The experience of left arm pain during a heart attack is a well-known example of referred pain. The nerves from the heart and the arm both arrive at the same part or 'segment' of the spinal cord, so the heart and arm are said to be 'segmentally related'. During a heart attack, the intense and prolonged pain sensations from the heart switch on all the nerves in that segment of the spinal cord, including those of the arm. The brain then experiences pain in both the heart and the arm.

Mechanical disorders cause referred pain to travel to many parts of the body. The lower back is well recognised as a source of referred pain to the groin, hip and thigh. Tense upper neck muscles, as explained above, might refer pain over the head. Hip troubles can affect the knee, while the neck and upper back can refer pain down the arm.

Referred pain is deceptive when there is little or no pain at the source of trouble, as can be the case. Fortunately, problems that typically cause referred pain are fairly well understood, so we can usually locate the real problem. More often, referred pain is accompanied by pain at the source of the trouble and this draws attention to itself.

> An aching knee is quite a common story of referred pain. My own daughter Lara, aged 9 at the time, complained of an aching left knee. Initially I didn t take much notice. Pretending to be a good practitioner, I bent the knee up and down a few times, noted there was nothing amiss and told her: There you are. All better . I expected it to pass and to be forgotten as Lara continued her full and active childhood.
>
> A little while later, Lara again said her knee was aching. I was in a bit of a hurry and gave it much the same approach. When she complained yet again I realised that Lara was feeling genuine discomfort and there was a problem that needed to be taken more seriously. On examination, her knee and hip were perfectly OK. But when I came to examine her lower back, I found she had thickened, hard and fibrous muscles and tenderness on the left side in the small of her back, and that one joint was decidedly stiff. The findings indicated a

longstanding problem on the side and part of the back that refers pain to the left knee. This was clearly the source of her knee pain.

Suddenly, I recalled seeing Lara aged 4 fall from her bed and land heavily and awkwardly on the small of her back across a low wooden stool. At the time she was crying in pain and hurting badly. But after soothing her pain and gently examining her back all appeared to be fine and the incident seemed to be forgotten in a few days. We thought no more about it. Five years later, this was surely the reason for the tissue changes I could feel.

Lara had a classic case of an old injury causing referred pain. The original injury had left scar tissue and stiffness. Now, Lara s recent physical activities were overloading the scar tissue, causing strain and referring pain to her left knee. Thankfully, a few manual therapy sessions fixed the lower back and relieved the knee symptoms, which have not reappeared since. This is still a talking point with Lara, who remembers and well understands the mechanism of referred pain. And I learnt to take my family s musculoskeletal problems more seriously!

Reflex effects

Referred pain affects the 'sensory' message of pain going to the brain, whereas reflexes concern 'motor' messages to contract a muscle or stimulate sweat glands going to the body. They are somewhat similar as both are involuntary and, in mechanical problems, they occur together, although the signals travel in different directions.

Reflexes are usually thought of as an involuntary jump like a knee jerk. In this examination, tapping the tendon in front of the knee with a plexor (patella hammer) slightly stretches the thigh muscle. The nerves in the muscle send a message off to the spinal cord. Here they are connected to nerves that return to the muscle, causing it to contract briefly, making the knee jump.

Reflexes control nearly all bodily functions. For example, reflexes affected by a range of stimuli control your heart rate; they include oxygen and carbon dioxide levels, pain and emotional excitements. Blood pressure, digestion, sweating, shivering and eye focusing are similar and are all controlled by reflexes.

Mechanical disorders always trigger reflexes. Protective spasm of the back muscles in response to a strained back is a reflex event. Even a muscle nowhere near an injury can be tensed to some extent. Like referred pain, the tensed muscle merely has to be 'segmentally related'; that is, supplied by nerves from the same part of the spinal cord that has received the pain signals. For example, the second lumbar joint in the lower back is segmentally related to the muscle in the front of the thigh. So when a person injures this joint in the back, apart from suffering muscle spasm in their back — the body's response to protect the injury — they might notice their thigh muscle also becomes slightly tense.

Reflexes also stimulate sweat glands and blood vessels in the segmentally related region, so the skin of the thigh becomes both a little sweaty and slightly cold. This may go unnoticed for many reasons, but the reflex can easily be demonstrated with sensitive instruments.

Functional disorders

Most medical conditions of the chest and abdomen require medical attention. For example, kidney stones, stomach ulcer, hernia, heart attack and lung cancer are all medical conditions. They all have pathology (abnormal cells and tissues) that can be seen at the site of the problem. Stones are found within the kidney, an ulcer develops within the stomach lining, a hernia protrudes through a weak layer of muscle, a heart attack damages heart muscle, and cancer cells can be seen within the lung. Medical treatment is directed to the organ concerned. Manual therapy has no real role in the treatment of medical conditions.

However, sometimes a doctor can find no apparent reason for a disturbance in an organ or body part. This frustrating problem is given the slightly vague name of a 'functional disorder'. There is a problem in the way the part functions or behaves but there is no discernible disease to explain it. Doctors generally consider psychological issues such as anxiety, mental tension, fatigue and exhaustion to be the major source of functional problems.

Manual practitioners have a different explanation for some of these cases. They don't always accept that the origins are psychological. Instead, they may find a mechanical disorder in the back that causes an organ to misbehave. They claim that referred pain and reflexes from a back problem can combine to be the reason for a functional disorder. This connection between the back and the organs is called a 'somatovisceral reflex' (body to viscera reflex); it is well known to physiologists.

Referred pain to an organ can feel sharp, aching, nauseous, heavy or cramp-like. It can give alarming abdominal pains, chest and breast pain or period-like pains.

Reflex effects might include abdominal swelling, increased urinary frequency, difficult breathing, heart palpitations, oesophageal reflux (heartburn), and food that gets stuck behind the breastbone when swallowed. The muscular organs of the body are particularly prone to reflex overactivity. The digestive tract, uterus, bladder and heart are notorious for misbehaving when nothing can be found wrong.

Together, referred pain and reflex effects can imitate problems such as reflux (heartburn), gastritis, hiatus hernia, ulcer, gallstones, appendicitis, dysmenorrhoea (painful periods), enuresis (bed wetting), asthma, angina, heart irregularities and pleurisy. Some cases of irritable bowel syndrome may have a mechanical origin. The brain and nervous system have no way of distinguishing between a functional and a real problem. It is as though there is really something wrong inside.

Osteopaths and chiropractors have had more than 100 years of experience with mechanical disorders. Although research evidence is still lacking, anecdotal successes suggest that the thoracic spine is a common, unrecognised source of minor ailments and disturbed function of the organs. It is in the area of functional disorders that manual practitioners believe mechanical problems are underestimated by mainstream medicine. For many of these cases, manual therapy can provide a simple and appropriate means of treatment.

Functional problems account for only a small part of the case load of osteopaths and chiropractors, although we suspect some sufferers never ask for help because a back problem is not obvious to them or their medical practitioner. In many cases, manual therapy may be able to relieve their suffering when orthodox medicine has not. (See Chapter 14, Abdominal functional disturbance.)

The role of manual therapy in symptoms at a distance

Referred pain and reflex effects, including those that combine to give functional problems in the chest and abdomen, tend to occur when the mechanical problem is more deeply located or longstanding, even if the symptoms are recent.

Fortunately, manual therapy works well in both deep and long-established problems. Recovery may be a little slower than for problems which have only just appeared, taking three or four treatments before there is clear evidence of progress. Even if you are lucky enough to experience immediate improvement, you should remember that longstanding problems do recover more gradually. If you discontinue treatment too soon, symptoms can re-establish themselves and you might have to resume treatment.

Manual practitioners are trained to identify functional disorders affecting the organs and to distinguish them from medical diseases of the chest and abdomen, which require treatment from a medical practitioner. We are very conscious of the possibility of other diseases being present and alert to the need to refer the client on for further tests or back to their medical practitioner.

Mechanical disorders and medical diseases

The role of the spine in real conditions of the abdomen and chest, such as an ovarian cyst, diverticulitis or cystic fibrosis, or in general medical diseases affecting the body, such as diabetes or leukaemia, has been an area of great dispute between orthodox medicine and osteopathy and chiropractic.

The early pioneers of manual therapy would treat anything. In the late 19th century, Doctors Still and Palmer, the founders of osteopathy and chiropractic, both felt they had made a shattering breakthrough for mankind. Indeed, they claimed surprisingly good results in many conditions. Influenza, eczema, gallstones, appendicitis, angina and pleurisy were all in a day's work. Like other zealots, they were undeterred by failure and simply believed they had not found the correct bone to push. At that time, medicine was often little better, especially in the snake oil world of the

American Midwest where both lived after the American Civil War.

It seems plain enough now that Doctors Still and Palmer did not have all the answers and that aspects of their discovery and claims were quite wrong. After all, spinal problems do not cause pathology (abnormal changes in tissues and cells), or disease in the arms and legs, so why should they do so in the organs of the body?

As there has been a total lack of evidence to support their theories, most osteopaths and chiropractors have come to accept that spinal problems do not cause real diseases in the chest and abdomen. They do know that organ nerves can be stimulated to produce symptoms that mimic disease. Known neurophysiological mechanisms quite adequately explain the connection between the spine and the problems we call functional disorders.

But there still remains a small area of mystery. Treating the spine does occasionally seem to alleviate symptoms in real visceral disease. It appears that the back sometimes affects such medical conditions as gastritis, diverticulitis and gallstones. There are two possible reasons for the occasional relationship: double diagnosis and misdiagnosis.

Double diagnosis

A double diagnosis occurs when a patient has two problems at the same time. Double diagnoses are actually not uncommon, particularly when one of them is musculoskeletal, as happens quite frequently. Although manual practitioners treat only a small group of conditions out of the several thousand conditions treated by doctors, this small group accounts for 10–20 per cent of visits to a doctor. Mechanical problems are therefore very common, so it is inevitable that from time to time the symptoms of a musculoskeletal problem will overlap and double up with a medical problem.

For example, a back problem might give referred pain and reflexes to the abdomen, overlapping with and adding to the symptoms of a medical condition already present in the abdomen. The two problems together can confuse and mislead a diagnostician who is only on the lookout for one condition. What is more, overlapping symptoms seem to be more pronounced when they occur together as opposed to separately. Remove one set of symptoms and the overall picture can improve dramatically.

You might be able to tell if this is occurring. Say your chest or abdominal complaint is being managed by your doctor, but you both feel the symptoms seem different, out of place, or more widespread, persistent or pronounced than they should be. If you also feel achey, tense, tired, tender or stiff between the shoulder blades or have had previous back trouble, a manual practitioner might identify a mechanical problem here. Manual therapy can help the back complaint and remove the symptoms that have been referred to the chest or abdomen. In this case, the back problem has been adding to the internal complaint and magnifying the intensity of its symptoms.

It should be stressed that this relationship happens only occasionally. You should discuss it with your medical practitioner and perhaps have a short trial of manual therapy. Three or four visits should be sufficient to demonstrate whether there is a connection and you are on the right track.

The relationship between visceral (chest and abdominal) disease and a back problem also works in reverse. Some visceral diseases cause pain and tension in the back muscles.

Gallstones, stomach ulcers, kidney ailments, appendicitis and abdominal aortic aneurysm are all capable of this trick. Manual practitioners are very conversant with referred pain and reflexes, and we are alert to this as a possibility. If it were suspected, you would be referred for medical evaluation and treatment.

Misdiagnosis

Human error may explain why treating the back can seem to cure a medical problem in the chest or abdomen. In this instance, the problem has been misdiagnosed in the first place and the manual practitioner has compounded the confusion by failing to recognise the mistake. The problem was never an organ disease at all, but a back problem giving referred and reflex effects to the abdomen.

This mistake was probably a good deal more common in the past than it would be these days. Medicine in the first half of the 20th century bore little resemblance to what we know today. With limited education and diagnostic technology, doctors of the day probably misdiagnosed a large number of mechanical complaints with referred and reflex effects as 'a spot of angina', 'a touch of pleurisy', 'a few gallstones' or 'a small ulcer'. When the problem didn't respond to medical treatment, some of these patients found their way to a manual practitioner who would examine their back, as was their way, and discover the real reason for the pain. After successful treatment, the manual practitioner was happy to accept the incorrect diagnosis and claim credit for curing it.

Medical practitioners would recognise that this type of diagnostic dilemma occurs even today. For example, pain in the cheek or forehead may be misdiagnosed as sinusitis when the real culprit is a tension headache referred from the upper neck. Similarly, dizziness is often ascribed to ear troubles such as labyrinthitis, a virus or Meniere's disease, when the real and more common cause of dizziness is cervical (neck) vertigo. Chest wall pain, referred from the back, may be mistaken for pleurisy, while persistent abdominal symptoms coming from the back might be diagnosed as irritable bowel syndrome.

Is there more to manual therapy?

There was a time when both osteopathy and chiropractic claimed that every medical condition was caused by bony blockage to the flow of blood and 'nerve-force'. With the decline of this belief, most osteopaths and chiropractors have become practitioners specialising in the treatment of backache and musculoskeletal symptoms. These clinicians rationalise manual therapy along conventional orthopaedic and mechanical grounds.

However, there are many chiropractors and osteopaths who remain attached to their roots. They say that their form of 'real' chiropractic or osteopathy is 'so much more' than the manual therapy practised by their colleagues. What this 'so much more' is in the way of therapeutic power is not well specified. These clinicians claim that their palpatory diagnosis and manual treatment skills can help conditions which their colleagues have relinquished to medicine.

They may argue the concept of predisposition. Exposed to the same risk, why do some people develop a chest infection, gastritis or other diseases while others do not? There are many reasons for the difference, including genetics and immunity, and the dietary, physical and mental health of the body. These practitioners theorise that reflexes arising from spinal problems might predispose people to a disease, so everyone should have a manual therapy check-up to lower his or her risk.

Some clinicians use newer manual methods of diagnosis and treatment. For example, cranial manual therapy and applied kinesiology are both diagnostic and therapeutic techniques that are claimed to widen the scope of manual therapy.

Others say some medical conditions have physical barriers created by inflammation, congestion and scar tissue, which limit fluid exchange and healthy tissues. Manual therapy is said to reduce these barriers, promote fluid exchange, flush out wastes and provide a fresh environment for the cells to operate in. Manual therapy is said to enhance cellular activity and optimise recovery in medical conditions.

Some practitioners are not really sure where they stand; they would like to sit on the fence in case some new evidence crops up. Until then, they say they want to treat the same conditions seen by medical practitioners and decide for themselves whether or not manual therapy is appropriate. They may think that the evidence-based rationalists specialising in backache and mechanical problems in the arms and legs, have closed minds and are missing out.

However, the evidence-based rationalists don't miss out, and are no less skilled in palpation or treatment — they just see things differently. They help exactly the same mechanical problems but without giving unrealistic hope that manual therapy can somehow affect or cure medical conditions. They make a clearer distinction between mechanical problems and medical conditions. The mechanical problem generally responds well, whereas a medical condition is far more unpredictable and often has limited response.

Whatever the rationale for a wider scope to manual therapy, there is scant evidence to back up their claims that manual therapy can fix everything. Osteopaths and chiropractors use manual therapy for very few conditions other than those with mechanical findings. Studies show that mechanical disorders represent at least 98 per cent of conditions treated by osteopaths in Britain and chiropractors in Scandinavia. So although some might wish for the wider role of bygone days, increased knowledge and better education has irreversibly changed manual practices.

Moreover, the people who seek our skills already seem to have decided the matter for us. They only come for the mechanical conditions they have discovered and know we can help. It seems that the public already has us rounded up and headed in the right direction.

It will be some time before we can be absolutely certain of the limits to manual therapy. Until then, practitioners will continue to speculate until enough research has settled the questions.

CHAPTER FOUR

RESPONSES TO TREATMENT

- Reactions ■ Unusual reactions
- Progress in longstanding problems
- Scepticism isn t always healthy
- Minimising reactions

Most patients find manual therapy to be comfortable, relaxing and just what is needed, particularly since manual therapists are trained to use minimum force. However, quite often it does appear that what we do makes the problem temporarily worse. This relates to a special category of symptoms that we call treatment reaction, treatment soreness or retracing (the sense of symptom reversal during recovery). A reaction is akin to a side effect of medication; it is a common, less desirable effect along the road to recovery. Reactions or side effects such as soreness and tiredness occur frequently and are considered quite normal, but they can be important and must be treated with respect to avoid a reaction that could be even greater.

Reactions

Individual responses vary, but about two-thirds of the people who come to see a manual practitioner have an immediate sense of improvement, with symptoms reducing uneventfully over the following hours or days. The other one-third develop some sort of mild but short-lived treatment reaction lasting 12 to 24 hours, although it can sometimes last up to

48 hours. Here you feel an immediate improvement followed by a reaction two to four hours later. There appear to be two components to this reaction.

Firstly, you might feel quite tired, as if you've had a long day or a hard game of sport. Fatigue seems more pronounced when the problem relates to widespread muscular tension. If you have a rest, you may be surprised that you fall asleep in the middle of the day. That night you might sleep quite heavily and wake refreshed the next morning. Although unproven, there is a theory that the sense of tiredness may be related to the waste metabolites (chemicals) in contracting muscles, which have been flushed out by the therapy into the circulation.

Secondly, you might feel tender or sensitive. Your symptoms might feel worse and have a bruised sensation. This discomfort is due to the therapeutic trauma of treatment causing an inflammatory reaction. It is the same as the ache you feel after a visit to the dentist when a tooth has been drilled out and filled. The mild discomfort is, in a way, reassuring because it means that the site of the injury has been properly identified. True bruising is unusual, although you should inform your practitioner if you do bruise easily so that extra care can be taken. Bruising results from blood leaking out of damaged capillaries into the spaces between the cells. Practitioners are careful to avoid this mishap.

If several areas are treated at the same time, a person can ache and feel slightly ill, as though he or she has the flu. Sometimes these effects develop overnight to surprise you the following morning.

Unusual reactions

Manual treatment can lead to unexpected reactions. There are several possible reasons, but if you are concerned it is best to phone your practitioner. In most cases there is a simple explanation.

A reaction is more likely after the first or second session and we do take a little more care at this time. This is when the injury is at its worst, with maximum spasm, inflammation and concentration of wastes, so the tissues are slightly more fragile and likely to react.

You might increase your discomfort by overexerting yourself after treatment or by simply continuing with a busy and tiring day. Occasionally the reaction can be alarming, particularly if you are absorbed in activity and don't realise how involved you are. Some people are lulled into a false sense of security and pay the penalty; they feel so good they try to complete the task in the garden or the home that originally caused the injury.

A person who has difficulty attending an appointment, perhaps because of distance or work commitments, might have a long interval between visits. In some cases, the practitioner might deliberately choose to give a slightly more intensive treatment. If this is the case, you will be warned to expect a little more treatment reaction than is usual.

Recovery is slower if you're tired, run down or burnt out. Therapy ultimately relies on the body's own healing abilities, so you might have to reduce your commitments and be more considerate towards yourself.

Emotional stress can be the reason for pain and it can also prevent recovery. In some cases, the pain is due to a prolonged negative life situation and will not respond to manual therapy at all. This pain is not mechanical; it's cause lies in the person's life circumstances.

On the other hand, when the person is feeling downcast because of a painful mechanical problem, something quite different occurs. As the problem improves, the mild depression also lifts. Neck disorders seem to have a particular capacity to cause a sense of 'flatness' or mild depression. This might be recognised only after the problem resolves.

It is also true that some reactions can be due to an over-enthusiastic practitioner. If this happens you should advise the practitioner how you felt afterwards so that he or she can modify the treatment and, if appropriate, review the diagnosis. It is not always easy to judge at the first visit exactly how much treatment should be applied. Even the best practitioners occasionally over-treat patients. It rarely happens more than once; after all, it is in the interests of both parties to have a satisfied and happy client. So don't give up on a practitioner just because of one undesirable treatment reaction. Tell them how you felt and give them another chance to get it right.

As a general rule, reactions lasting more than 48 hours are neither intended nor beneficial. If the reason for the reaction is unclear, contact your practitioner.

Progress in longstanding problems

Most people expect a mechanical problem to recover like any other common ailment, with a steady and progressive reduction of symptoms. It should behave like a cold, a graze or a bruise. Pain, the most important measure of a mechanical problem, does indeed usually recover in this way when the injury is recent. However, a chronic (longstanding) problem is more deeply entrenched and pain rarely reduces steadily without interruption. If you measure progress here by pain alone, you might initially doubt whether there has been any improvement at all. It helps to know that this is quite normal and that you are not alone in this experience.

However, there are usually some signs of improvement, even after the very first session. At the very least, the practitioner will feel some difference when they palpate the area, but most patients will also detect small but important signs of recovery.

After the first treatment, the main change is a sense of increased looseness or improved flexibility of the problem region. This might be present without any apparent reduction of pain. You will feel less stiff in the morning and will be able to stand up from a sitting position or get out of the car and move off more easily.

After the next session the pain becomes more localised; the central discomfort may be just as bad, but the more peripheral and lesser symptoms will reduce or disappear.

Following the third session, the pain starts to become more intermittent. The core pain may be as bad as ever when it is present, but you will find there are increasing periods of relief. The pain will be more localised, and the area will feel looser.

Then, after the fourth treatment, you will start to smile as you recognise a reduction in the intensity of discomfort. Pain, the main measure of the problem, is finally beginning to subside.

So people with a longstanding mechanical problem should look for more subtle changes along the way rather than an instant reduction in pain levels. The steps of improved flexibility, greater localisation and more frequent periods of relief will usually precede real easing of the pain.

If the problem is not so entrenched, this sequence can be compressed over two or three visits, while more longstanding cases may extend over five or six visits before a clear and sustained reduction in pain is felt.

Sometimes the symptoms might simply change or pain might develop in a different location. These are not necessarily bad signs and they can indicate progress in a stubborn problem.

Occasionally, a surprising oscillation develops. Immediately following treatment the patient feels better. After two or three hours a treatment reaction develops, lasting up to 24 hours. As this subsides, the patient again feels improved. Then after a few days, the benefits of the therapy wear off and symptoms return to some extent. Finally, because the treatment has provided sufficient impetus to healing, a gradual reduction of symptoms becomes apparent. This means that a single therapy session can make symptoms better, then worse, then better, then worse, and finally better again. So fluctuations are not necessarily a concern; they can be a normal part of the healing cycle.

It is one of my biggest pleasures when a client says: 'Do

you know, it did exactly what you predicted it would?' He or she is clearly impressed and well on their way to recovery.

Scepticism isn't always healthy

Healthy scepticism is a very useful tool for assessing the quality of any care. You should feel positive and supported, and cautious of bold and unrealistic claims. There is poor advice in every area of healthcare; *caveat emptor* applies — the buyer should always beware.

At the same time, scepticism can contribute to the problem. Over-cautious people, sometimes on medical advice, are more likely to avoid manual treatment until they are desperate and the problem is well entrenched. Some people don't know who to go and see and avoid doing anything. Others are unnecessarily dubious about treatment, and sometimes abandon a course of treatment too early. So if you are a 'doubting Thomas', be prepared to give the treatment a little more time to work than you believe is necessary. Then be sure to discuss your options with your practitioner before deciding whether or not to continue treatment. Do remember that two-way communication is a vital part of receiving sound advice. Continuing treatment for just a little longer, with one or two more visits, can be decidedly better than some other options. A trial of three or four treatments is usually enough to demonstrate whether or not you are on the right track.

Minimising reactions

Adequate rest is important. Do too much too soon and you can feel as if you were never treated at all. Generally you should avoid treatment before you plan to do something strenuous or prolonged.

We usually advise people to take it quietly for 24 hours

after treatment. If possible, rest for an hour or two later in the day. Have a soak in the bath or under a hot shower before going to bed a little earlier than usual, perhaps half to one hour sooner. An alcoholic drink is quite a helpful muscle relaxant. One is enough; more may be merrier but it's not therapeutically necessary.

For those who don't object to medication, it is helpful to take an aspirin or some other anti-inflammatory within two hours of treatment and again later in the day or last thing at night. As well as relieving the discomfort of the problem, it will assist in relaxing muscle spasm and reduce stiffness and inflammation; it helps the treatment to be more effective.

Many people attending manual practitioners are already taking anti-inflammatory (aspirin-like) medication prescribed by their medical practitioner. They should continue to follow the medical advice or check with their doctor whether they should continue, but generally the medication can be reduced as the symptoms subside.

BONES AND JOINT CRACKING

CHAPTER FIVE

- The great bone out of place controversy
- The question of joints
- Why is the explanation still current?
- The crack
- A variety of diagnoses

In the past, manual practitioners believed that manipulation worked by pushing misaligned bones back into place. Many practitioners, even now, tell their patients that their problem centres around a bone that's out of place. Most members of the public, if asked, would probably say that bones can become out of place!

Unfortunately this concept is no longer accepted. More and more, it is becoming recognised that it is the soft tissues that are both the source of symptoms and the recipients of any treatment. Bones just happen to be attached by soft tissue. The purpose of pushing and pulling on the bones is to treat the soft tissues attached to them. Mechanical disorders rarely alter the relationship between two bones. Small irregularities of bone alignment are normal, frequent and widespread throughout the body. They do not cause symptoms, they do not need attention; they are simply natural variations of the skeletal framework.

The great 'bone out of place' controversy

It is easy to understand why the misalignment theory arose in the first place. The idea is as old as Hippocrates. A dislocated joint was pulled out of its socket; it seemed logical that a less drastic problem was simply a smaller degree of dislocation, a subluxation (mechanical problem) or misalignment.

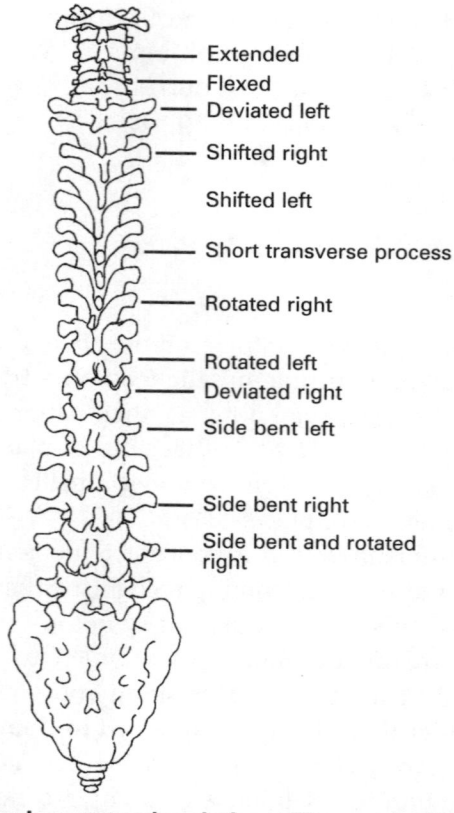

- Extended
- Flexed
- Deviated left
- Shifted right
- Shifted left
- Short transverse process
- Rotated right
- Rotated left
- Deviated right
- Side bent left
- Side bent right
- Side bent and rotated right

Normal spine showing minor natural variations. These misalignments were incorrectly thought to be the mechanical disorders (subluxations) that manual practitioners treated.

Even the name 'bonesetter', the term for manual practitioners of yesteryear, was derived from the idea that bones can move out of place. The 'setting' meant re-alignment of the bones, similar to setting the teeth on a saw when sharpening its blade. It did not refer to the hardening of a plaster of Paris splint around a broken bone. Bonesetters were the community's manual practitioners.

Early on in the development of the manual professions, both osteopaths and chiropractors thought that manipulation moved errant bones back into place. The theory corresponded with their palpation experiences. The bone felt misplaced.

The theory also makes sense to the sufferer. A 'crick' in the neck, back, knee or some other joint creates a sense of misplacement. The 'proprioceptive' nerves that tell us the position of our joints, even when our eyes are closed, are stimulated and trick the brain. It really feels as if a bone is out of line. After feeling a click of manipulation, the reduction in proprioceptive stimulation, together with comfort and ease of movement, gives a very real sense of realignment.

The advent of X-rays about a century ago finally seemed to provide proof-positive that bones can become misaligned. Minor irregularities of alignment, increasingly accepted as normal, were found over the whole skeleton, and appeared to confirm the centuries-old theory. It was only a matter of picking the irregularity nearest the patient's symptoms and showing them the 'problem' on X-ray.

But the theory started to unravel. As our understanding of mechanical disorders increased, we discovered some inconvenient and contradictory evidence. The details simply weren't right.

Manual therapy cannot help bone disease. For example, bone tumour, osteoporosis (bone thinning), Paget's disease (thickened and deformed bones), periostitis (bony bruising) and fracture are all bone conditions that are unaffected by and unsuited to manual treatment, which might even be dangerous.

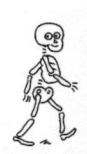

When we palpate the soft tissues, their textures closely reflect the length of time a problem has been present. Inflammation and muscle tension is felt in a recent problem, while harder, more fibrous tissue textures are felt in a longstanding problem. As the symptoms subside we can feel, through palpation, an exactly matching recovery in the soft tissues without change in the bones.

Helen hobbled into the practice with an acutely strained ankle. The previous evening, while returning to her car from the theatre in the rain, she had slipped on the steps and had gone over on the outside of her ankle. When examined, Helen s ankle was not only swollen with a puffy, congested feel, but also highly sensitive to touch. Helen did not like the gentle manual testing of her injury. Movement was limited and painful when I turned her foot inwards, and the leg muscles tensed up in protest at the slightest movement. Her injury was clearly recent.

In contrast, Anne, a keen skier, fell badly on Mt Buller two years ago and her right ankle, which was not treated at the time, had never fully recovered. Whenever she tried to run with her dog or spent a day in town shopping, the outside of her ankle would bother her. This ankle injury gave a totally different impression to Helen s. The ankle joint was stiff in every direction, particularly when the foot was turned outward. There was not much swelling but I could feel a thickened, hard, fibrous ligament on the outside of the ankle. The lower leg muscles had a similar sense of firm, fibrous lack of elasticity and life. My fingers confirmed Anne s story: this was a longstanding problem.

These two cases demonstrate some of the differences between recent and longstanding soft tissue injuries.

Pain is another piece of evidence; it's felt in the soft tissues, not the bones. And when a finger pressure is applied to the faulty soft tissues, the person feels their characteristic pain right there under the finger.

In practice, we are not feeling misaligned bones. Instead, we are sensing the soft tissues that control the flexibility of the joints. A mechanical problem gives a manual practitioner the feeling of a misplaced bone only because the joint opposes motion. The bony resistance and obstruction to motion creates an illusion that a bone is out of place. This has tricked manual practitioners for years.

More detailed X-ray studies have clinched the argument, showing clear visual proof. It can be seen that in healthy people the bones of the spine are only approximately in line. In other words, bones are frequently slightly misaligned. What's more, X-rays taken before and after manipulation very rarely show any change in alignment. In reality, misalignments are normal and natural variations in skeletal architecture, and not problems that need our attention and treatment.

When we take an X-ray to show the bones, it does not reveal the very tissues that are the real source of mechanical symptoms. The simple truth is that manual therapy does not treat the bones. They are no more than levers used to apply therapeutic forces to the attached soft tissues.

The question of joints

While the true role of the soft tissues is undergoing investigation and increasing recognition, the debate has been prolonged, complicated and confused by conditions that affect both bones and soft tissues.

Joint diseases, by definition, involve both the bones and the soft tissues connecting them. They include problems like osteoarthritis (degeneration of joints), spondylosis (degeneration of the spine), Scheuermann's disease (defective growth of vertebrae in children), spondylolysis (vertebral stress fracture), disc degeneration and metatarsalgia (pain in the metatarsal bones of the foot). However, in all these cases the bones are not affected by manual therapy; improvement is made and felt only in the nearby attached soft tissues.

For example, a bony spur might pinch a nerve and cause pain, but if manual therapy relieves the pain, the spur is still there. The treatment only reduces the pressure of swollen tissues squeezing the nerve within its narrowed margins. Reduce the inflammation and the nerve might pass through its narrowed confines without complaint.

Osteoarthritis is another example. X-rays of the bones before and after manual therapy to relieve pain and improve flexibility look exactly the same. Manual therapy has no effect on osteoarthritic bones; it only restores the soft tissues joining the bones to their previous pain-free state.

In many mechanical disorders the bone itself seems painful. This tenderness is not due to an abnormality of the bone, but rather to a muscle, a ligament or a joint capsule that is painful and happens to be attached to the bone. The tenderness resolves as the soft tissues recover.

Why is the explanation still current?

The concept of bone misalignment pressing on nerves is alive and well in many areas of manual therapy. It occurs mostly in chiropractic, although osteopaths and masseurs still use the idea, whereas medical practitioners and physiotherapists sensibly avoid the misalignment debate. The prefix osteo- in osteopathy, meaning bone, does not help the notion subside. The public certainly has a firm belief in it, presumably assisted by the explanations from manual practitioners.

Some people think that muscle spasm can pull a bone out

of line. But, we know from X-rays that this hardly ever happens and if it does it is certainly not with the frequency that 'misalignments' are said to occur. The numerous other tissues (disc, ligament, joint capsule, large muscles and bony apposition) joining the vertebrae prevent spasm of the small intervertebral muscles pulling a vertebra out of line.

Historically, chiropractors used misalignment as a key part of their system of explanation. A misalignment seen on an X-ray supported their theories. For example, a patient consulting a chiropractor might have X-ray films of their spine taken. On the X-rays, the patient is shown a misaligned vertebra, described as a subluxation, which is said to cause nerve interference. He or she is told that if the vertebra is adjusted to correct the subluxation, it will relieve the nerve interference. The inescapable but wrong conclusion is that a misplaced vertebra is pinching a nerve.

The idea of nerve interference developed from the old incorrect idea that a misaligned bone pinched nerves and, to fix the problem, the bone needed to be put back into place. These days nerve interference has a quite different and new meaning that is much closer to 'symptoms and signs'. Nerve interference describes every effect that a subluxation (mechanical problem) can have via the nervous system; it includes local and referred pain, muscle spasm, circulatory changes, sweating and more distant reflexes affecting the chest and abdominal viscera, as well as pressure on a nerve.

However, every single disease has effects on the nervous system, whether it is a viral infection, a heart attack, diabetes or a broken bone. A person with the flu might have a temperature, sore throat, running nose, sweats, cough, headache, and muscular aches and pains. The nervous system is involved in all of these processes, but instead of saying that the flu causes nerve interference, we prefer to say that the flu has certain symptoms and signs.

A chiropractor might say a subluxation is causing nerve interference, whereas another practitioner would say a joint has been strained, giving pain, muscle spasm and joint stiffness. The chiropractor is describing exactly the same thing, but the idea of misaligned bones pressing on nerves is deeply entrenched, particularly in the minds of older practitioners who were educated before the idea was disproved. The new concept will take time to pass down through the system.

In many ways, the concept of misalignment, although unfounded, is a convenient explanation. It is easy to describe to people. It helps to build a visual image that fits with a patient's sensation. It may continue to be used as popular terminology, just as the term 'slipped disc' has persisted despite our knowledge that discs do not slip in or out of place.

However, a wrong idea is still a wrong idea. Diagnostic accuracy is important and mistaken theories impede progress. The mental picture of misalignment obscures the truth. It is an idea whose time has passed.

The crack

Once we have eliminated the concept of misalignment, we can look again at the cracking sound of manipulation, which chiropractors call 'adjustment' and 'dynamic thrust', osteopaths call 'high velocity thrust' and 'mobilisation with impulse', and physiotherapists know as 'grade five mobilisation'.

This is the same noise as joint cracking in everyday life, a mysterious and sometimes anti-social activity. The sound of finger joints being cracked in succession can disturb and even sicken some people.

The crack is thought to be a process that physicists call cavitation. When the two halves of a joint are separated, low pressure within the joint causes synovial (joint) fluid to vaporise and gas to be released from solution. The vapour bubble collapses immediately and results in the cracking sound. The noise is an implosion crack similar to a light bulb popping or, in a simmering kettle, the sound of hundreds of bubbles collapsing as they rise to cooler levels.

The immediate relief following manipulation has nothing to do with a bone being realigned. It is more likely due to a reduction in painful muscle spasm and improved flexibility.

Any of the small joints in the body can be manipulated to give a crack or pop. It is not a bone slipping back into place or a disc repositioning itself or adhesions splitting apart. It is only a by-product of treatment and a physiological curiosity. The crack simply means the halves have been momentarily separated in a certain way. A manipulation that cracks a joint when it is intended may be slightly more useful but the absence of a crack does not mean the procedure has failed.

A manipulated joint may not crack for several reasons. A joint that has normal mobility does not crack as easily as a slightly stiff joint; it does not need manipulation. A very stiff joint is difficult to crack and it might be unsafe to apply too much force. The technique is then used to test whether it is ready to be manipulated or it is better to slightly stretch and loosen it without manipulation.

Some people like to crack their finger joints. They might discover that others find it distasteful and irritating. Some regard it as bad manners, similar to picking one's nose. The joint cracker might be told that repeated cracking will lead to osteoarthritis. At present there is no evidence to show that this view is either correct or incorrect. In some ways the idea that joint cracking causing arthritis runs against manual practitioners' experience that maintaining joint flexibility is healthy and will minimise future problems. Until there is more evidence, in my opinion joint cracking probably does no harm. 'Stop doing it, you'll get arthritis', may only be an old wives' tale in the same category as 'Stop doing it, you'll go blind'! If you like cracking your joints, perhaps it would be better to do it in private.

A variety of diagnoses

Historically, orthodox medicine has found back problems difficult to treat, so people with mechanical problems have often done the rounds of several different clinicians before consulting a manual practitioner.

This process can be bewildering for people, causing some to ask their manual practitioner to answer a few basic questions: 'Why do I get a different diagnosis from every person I see?' 'Which of these is correct?' 'Is the trouble very difficult to diagnose or have I got several different things wrong with me?'

Back pain is probably best managed by practitioners who see a large number of back pain patients. The special diagnostic tool of a manual practitioner is palpation, something medical practitioners are not specifically trained in. They do not have our manual therapy skills either. Although a medical practitioner might specialise in radiology, the soft tissues we treat do not show up well on X-ray pictures. Also, each practitioner develops his or her own personal form of explanation and the same problem might be given a variety of names. Manual practitioners have added to the confusion with each discipline having its own terminology and diagnoses.

A single problem might be described as lumbago, muscle

spasm, strained back, joint strain, arthritis, degeneration, bad posture, one short leg, curvature, subluxation, misalignment, lesion or somatic dysfunction. A suffering patient might be told that their disc is slipped, sprained, bulging, herniated, protruding, prolapsed, ruptured, narrowed, thinned, degenerated or disrupted! No wonder the old faithful 'slipped disc' remains popular. The chaos of labels can lead the sufferer to conclude that they are the victim of a constellation of disorders. Generally this is not true; the various diagnoses simply focus on different aspects of the same problem or just give it different names.

> Sacha, a 15-year-old only child, has two caring parents who worry whenever she is sick. Recently she complained of a pain in her back, which was preventing her from participating in her favourite sport of netball. Her GP told her everything was OK but Sacha still complained of a sore lower back. Her concerned parents decided to take her to the GP s partner, who is more interested in back problems. He suggested a CT scan and blood tests, but these came back as normal. The doctor diagnosed growing pains and suggested she avoid vigorous sport and try some gentle exercise such as swimming.
>
> Several weeks later, she was still suffering back pain and her parents were becoming increasingly anxious, so the doctor referred Sacha to a physiotherapist. The physiotherapist didn t believe in growing pains but told Sacha she has a curvature. He gave her heat treatment, massage and daily exercises to perform. But still poor Sacha was in pain. The next step was a referral to see an orthopaedic specialist, who naturally referred her for an MRI (magnetic resonance imaging) scan, after which he diagnosed a bulging disc and the prospect of possible surgery. Now Sacha and her parents were really scared. They had received a different answer from each practitioner and were not at all sure who was right.
>
> A good friend of Sacha s parents, and a patient of mine, advised them, Before taking drastic action, why not try some-

> thing less invasive . It was obvious when we met that Sacha and her parents were genuinely concerned about the different diagnoses they had received and were naturally a little wary.
> After examining Sacha I suggested she had a trial of three manual therapy sessions after which we would reassess the progress. Happily, I could focus manual therapy to the exact part of the lower back where her trouble was centred. Relaxing Sacha s tense muscles and loosening her stiff joints allowed her problem to resolve itself naturally. She soon felt more comfortable and was back to normal in a few weeks.

Here was a fine example of how the variety of diagnoses can result in unnecessary worry and might have led to unnecessary surgery.

The problem of multiple diagnoses is not confined to mechanical disorders. Any condition that is not well understood or that is difficult to treat will lead to the sufferer 'doing the rounds' and receiving a different description and treatment at each stop. It's just that our need for an explanation and consensus has outstripped our knowledge. As manual therapy becomes more evidence-based, our understanding, communication, language and management of mechanical disorders will become more standardised. This will benefit both patients and practitioners.

CHAPTER SIX

METHODS OF TREATMENT

- Massage ■ Articulation (stretching)
- Mobilisation ■ Manipulation ■ Adjustment
- Exercise ■ Traction ■ Shiatsu, acupressure and trigger points ■ Muscle energy technique
- Cranial manual therapy ■ Activator technique
- Applied kinesiology

Manual therapy works principally on problems in two kinds of soft tissue: muscles, and tissues made of collagen (ligament, joint capsule, disc, tendon and fascia) (see Chapter 2).

The most superficial and abundant tissues are muscle, each one enclosed in a tough bag of fascia. Muscles account for the bulk of soft tissues that we treat. Those that are near the surface of the skin are directly accessible and can be treated by a variety of massage techniques.

More deeply placed within the body are many small and inaccessible structures that are tucked in beside or behind the bones and joints. The spine in particular, with its many processes and articulating parts, hides numerous small connecting tissues that are quite out of reach to probing fingers. Any of these connecting tissues can suffer injury, inflammation or pain, and benefit greatly from a manual approach.

How can we target these small and inaccessible parts? This question is really important to manual practitioners.

Deep tissues can be reached and influenced through the bones. Just as movement between two bones is used to assess the state of the tissues connecting them, bones can be used as levers to effect treatment precisely to the smallest ligament, joint capsule, disc or muscle buried far below the skin's surface.

Basically, one bone is articulated in relation to another. When one bone is moved, the tissues connecting it to its neighbour are stretched or shortened. Any soft tissue structure connecting two bones can be felt and treated in this way. Mobilisation and manipulation techniques have a particular capacity to focus on the small, deep 'unisegmental' soft tissues bridging two bones.

Although individual practitioners will favour different methods and apply them in various ways, we do tend to use a common kit of techniques. These tend to be deployed in a certain order. We work first on relaxing the overlying bulk of muscles using any one of the various forms of massage techniques. Shiatsu, traction and electrical treatments like ultrasound might also be useful. When overlying tension is sufficiently reduced, movement techniques such as articulation, mobilisation and manipulation localise treatment to the more deeply placed tissues inaccessible to manual probing.

Massage

Massage is the oldest, most widely applied and best known of our techniques. Everybody understands the benefits of massage. It relaxes the body and quietens a cluttered mind. Shoulders can ache after a long day's work, muscles become painful and sensitive after sport, and tension tends to build up in them when we are emotionally stressed. When you feel these sore areas with your fingertips they will be tender and hard. You may feel tight bands or firm knotted areas.

Manual therapists apply squeezing, stroking and stretching movements in each area to assist the exchange and cleaning processes of fluids around and within the muscle cells. Fresh nutrients replace stale wastes; restoring chemical balance creates relaxation, recovery and a stronger, more resilient body.

Some practitioners describe 'toxins' that have built up in the tissues. These toxins are not poisons like snakebite or arsenic or plants such as deadly nightshade. Toxins in the vocabulary of complementary practitioners usually refer to the normal waste products that come from cellular activity. When the waste products are in sufficient quantities they are believed to become toxic and affect the cellular workings of the body. Muscle cells in particular produce large quantities of waste chemicals. At times of continuous muscular tension, the wastes are said to be toxic and irritate pain nerve endings. Massage is a way of flushing away toxic wastes.

Professional massage techniques

- *Kneading* (petrissage, cross-fibre massage) consists of rhythmic pushing, grasping and squeezing sections of muscle, such as those on either side of the mid-line in the back. Muscle is kneaded like dough in order to relax hard, tense muscles, stimulate blood flow and eliminate wastes. Kneading is one of the more common forms of massage used.
- *Stroking* (effleurage, drainage) involves long, light strokes moving towards the heart to promote venous and lymphatic drainage in both skin and underlying muscle. The palm, thumb or heel of the hand is stroked along the length of a muscle. Stroking is usually increased from very light to moderate pressure, progressively affecting deeper tissues as accumulated fluid is dispersed. When cream or oils are applied, stroking is the most frequently used massage technique.
- *Inhibition* (pressure, blanching, shiatsu) is slowly increased and decreased pressure, usually applied with the pad of the thumb, reinforced with the other hand, or the point of the elbow. This treatment might be given to relieve a sensitive or 'trigger' point, felt as a small, hard, sometimes gritty spot and often located deep in a muscle.

Inhibition may be another form of acupressure and shiatsu.
- *Friction* uses small amplitude, light rubbing with the thumb, fingers or heel of the hand. Friction may be applied to stimulate circulation and relieve congestion in a ligament (for example, at the knee), a tendon (for example, the shoulder), or a tendon sheath (for example, the wrist).
- *Percussion* (tapotement, clapping) consists of short, fast rhythmic strokes, performed with the sides or cupped palms of the hands on the chest, back, buttocks or any other large fleshy region. This can be used on people with chest conditions such as emphysema or asthma.

Specialised systems of massage

Massage therapists combine the above traditional massage techniques with others in a variety of combinations to produce several specialised systems of massage.
- *Remedial or therapeutic massage* is a common type of massage used to treat a specific muscular dysfunction. It is applied to a discrete problem or region of discomfort.
- *Relaxation or Swedish massage* is a smooth, flowing, more superficial massage applied to the whole body. It is used to promote general relaxation, improve circulation and range of motion. On a psychological and emotional level, its calming and soothing effects allow people to deal more constructively with everyday worries and problems.
- *Sports massage* has long been recognised as a helpful component of any serious training program. If done before and after sport it can help prevent and treat muscular injury, and also minimise stiffness and fatigue.
- *Aromatherapy* combines massage with the subtle medicinal and psychological effects of highly scented essences or essential oils to promote relaxation, harmony and balance. It is unclear to what extent aromatherapy oils

can provide help compared with the accepted benefits of massage. Common sense suggests that, at the very least, a scented atmosphere, pleasant surrounds, relaxing music and a comfortable table will contribute to mental and physical relaxation.
- *Rolfing or postural integration* is a deep, firm and more demanding form of massage that progressively moves from the outer muscles to the deeper layers closer to the bones. It is based on the beliefs of Ida Rolf that physical and psychological well-being are connected and can be restored by releasing fixations in the body structure.
- *Bowen technique* is a flicking or twanging by the thumb or fingers across tight muscle to produce relaxation and relief from pain. It was developed by Tom Bowen, an Australian football club masseur. He was said to treat 50 patients a day, most of whom only needed two or three visits. His incredible success rate and remarkable results are legendary.

Alternative manual techniques

There is also a group of manual techniques that rely on alternative healing theories. Some combine massage with religious elements and others with Eastern theories of energy flow and the balancing forces of Yin and Yang. They have their devotees, but they can't claim the same level of scientific acceptance as traditional massage.
- *Reiki* is more a system of spiritual healing than a manual therapy. In a typical Reiki treatment, the client lies down fully clothed and receives a 'laying on of hands' that transfers 'energy' or 'universal life force'. Personal energy, more vitality, resilience, deep relaxation and distance healing are some of the claimed benefits of Reiki.
- *Polarity balancing* is similar to Reiki in both theory and application. It has connections with Ayurveda, India's form of complementary medicine. Illness is said to be

caused by 'blockages' of the body's energy currents. By the 'laying on of hands', polarity balancing harmonises the body's energy flow, allowing a person to overcome their illness.
- *Reflexology or zone therapy* is thought to treat disorders of the body by massaging 'reflex points' in the feet. Illnesses are said to show up as tender spots in the feet corresponding to particular areas of the body. It is claimed that the massage unblocks energy channels, resulting in healing.

Articulation (stretching)

Articulation is the technical term for the homely act of stretching. When we're tired or tense, stretching reduces tightness in the muscles and joints, and brings a wave of well-being. Stretching is almost a reflex — we do it intuitively, virtually without thought. It's so natural we feel good just watching the family pet stretch out after a snooze.

Articulation, or therapeutic stretching, is similar but performed on your body by the practitioner. Here, we repeatedly take a joint through its range of movement, slightly bending it a little further each time as it allows.

The method can relax the large superficial muscles, as well as the deeper and less accessible structures connecting a joint. The lower back can be articulated by levering with the legs, the neck can be loosened by moving the head. If we use a finger as a fulcrum placed between two vertebrae, like the support under a seesaw, it helps to focus and accentuate the forces to the tissues connecting adjacent vertebrae.

For example, we can articulate, or bend sideways, the whole lower back or a single lumbar joint. With a person lying on one side with their knees and hips bent, we can bend the whole lumbar spine sideways just by lifting the ankles. To focus more bending to one joint, we place the fingers of the other hand on the back between two of its bony knobs. Then the legs, as before, are lifted upwards, while the fingers on the back push down to form a fulcrum or apex, like an upside down seesaw; this focuses more bending to that level.

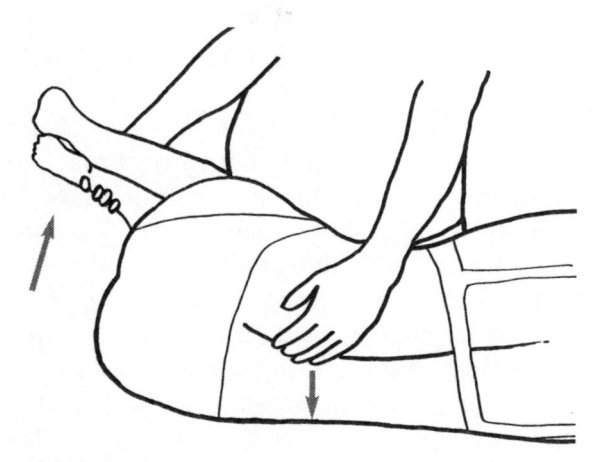

Lumbar side bending
(with permission C. Tucker in *Fundamental Osteopathic Technique*)

Mobilisation

Mobilisation uses rhythmic oscillations to restore movement to a joint. This technique uses small repeated pressures with the thumb or heel of the hand against some part of the vertebra to wobble it relative to its neighbour. It has most effect on the short, deep soft tissues that join a bone to its neighbour. It is one of the most useful ways of relaxing and freeing up the deep tissues that connect two bones.

Mobilisation is helpful by itself or it can be used as a stepping stone, to loosen and prepare a joint for manipulation. Mobilisation is popular because it is regarded as safe, comfortable, easy to apply and less dramatic than manipulation.

Geoff Maitland, an Australian physiotherapist, developed the idea of mobilisation. It is now a comprehensive method of treatment that is taught and practised worldwide. Physiotherapists in particular have concentrated on mobilisation, with many being highly skilled in its application.

Manipulation

Manipulation goes by many names, including joint cracking, mobilisation with impulse (osteopathy), adjustment (chiropractic), grade five mobilisation (physiotherapy), dynamic thrust (chiropractic) and high velocity low amplitude thrust (osteopathy).

We use the term here in its European meaning: to describe the precisely controlled impulse or thrust applied to a joint. In North America, the term manipulation may be used differently, as a global term for manual therapy or to indicate any manual technique at all.

Manipulation, like mobilising, has most effect on the short, deep tissues that join adjacent bones. It provides a momentary stretch of the 'unisegmental' tissues connecting two bones. It is often accompanied by a click, crack or pop. The technique seems to produce muscle relaxation, improved flexibility and diminished pain. The effect can be dramatic, the miracle cure, almost as if a bone has popped back into place. The noise of the pop or crack is believed to be associated with the collapse of a gas bubble formed within the joint cavity when the two halves are momentarily separated. (See Chapter 5, The crack.)

Manipulation is perhaps the most impressive manual technique, but many people tend to overrate its importance. Although it can cause an immediate benefit, it is much more often a brief step in several stages of treatment. It is most useful when pain, muscle spasm and stiffness are localised to precisely one joint. No well-trained manual practitioner uses undue force when manipulating a joint. (See Chapter 9, Dangers.)

Adjustment

Adjustment is a general term that describes any chiropractic treatment technique apart from massage, the nearest medical equivalent being 'manual therapy'. A chiropractic adjustment varies between the gentle oscillation of a joint, similar to a physiotherapist's mobilisation, to the more familiar joint cracking that manipulation is known for.

The general populace tend to use the term 'adjustment' slightly differently; they use it when speaking of manipulation (joint cracking) by a chiropractor. Manipulation is indeed one type of adjustment, but the term used by chiropractors for manipulation is 'dynamic thrust'.

A whole range of adjustments have been developed, packaged and made popular by influential practitioners and schools of chiropractic. They include the 'Gonsted' technique, where the patient is adjusted as they kneel, with their chest resting on a low table. 'Diversified' practitioners use a range of adjustment methods, hence the term 'diverse'. They are pragmatic and use whatever adjustment technique they consider appropriate to the job. The 'Activator' technique (see p. 95) is named after a small trigger gun (activator adjusting instrument) that is used to adjust a patient by delivering a small impact to one vertebra. The 'Nimmo' technique is a cross between acupressure and massage (see p. 92). The Palmer Package, a group of adjustive techniques, is named after the largest school of chiropractic. Some of the individual adjustments well known within the chiropractic profession include chrone upper cervical, toggle recoil, hole in one, drop-piece and torque release technique.

Exercise

Exercise benefits every part of your body; it is an important means of improving and maintaining your health. Your body thrives on exercise and it is important that you stay active in order to remain healthy.

There are three types of exercise, each with different benefits. Some exercises improve joint mobility and keep you supple, some increase muscular strength and increase endurance, while others that make you breathless and improve your heart and circulatory fitness. In addition, regular exercise gives you stronger bones and releases natural chemicals that reduce pain.

Of particular interest to manual practitioners is the effect of exercise on mobility and strength. We often recommend therapeutic exercises to be carried out between sessions or as a self-treatment to prevent minor recurrences or help the healing process. Although exercises can improve both mobility and strength, the effect can be tuned by selecting the range of motion or the degree of effort.

> Jolyon, aged 22, damaged the lateral cartilage of his right knee when he landed heavily on one heel while playing volleyball. Unfortunately it happened while he was overseas. He was advised that an operation was necessary. As he was due to return to Melbourne a week later he chose to wait until then before doing anything. Jolyon rested the knee as much as possible, wearing a brace and using crutches to move about. The physiotherapist explained how the quadriceps muscle in the front of the thigh wastes and looses strength very quickly when a cartilage is injured. It would therefore be helpful to his post-operative recovery to maintain the strength of the knee if possible. Jolyon was shown an exercise to tighten and strengthen the muscle while avoiding painful movement of the knee.

In manual therapy, joint stiffness is one of the key signs of mechanical trouble, and this does make us particularly interested in mobility. Muscular weakness, on the other hand, is sometimes misunderstood.

A person with a troublesome back might say he or she has a weak back when the muscles are actually well developed and strong. Instead, their 'weakness' is really a susceptibility to injury and pain due to some previous back trouble. Fix the trouble with manual therapy and the 'weakness' disappears, with or without strengthening exercises. In other cases, muscular weakness is due to pain preventing a strong contraction. The strength returns as soon as the pain resolves, again with or without the help of strengthening exercises.

It is important to note that strength does play a crucial role in protecting joints. If your muscles are strong and have endurance you are less likely to injure a joint. Weak muscles give less protection and allow more strain to be placed on the ligament supports. Weak and fatigued muscles can lead to a sprained joint, for example, at the ankle joint.

To maintain strength and endurance, you need to do appropriate exercises on a regular basis — stop and you begin to deteriorate immediately. Flexibility is different; once it has been restored, the range of motion in the joint is likely to stay that way.

Some mechanical problems are difficult to treat with exercise, particularly in the spine. Because it works as a flexible system, we can't exercise one stiff back joint on its own. Instead, the spine finds other ways to move, so if we try to loosen up one stiff spinal joint by exercising the part of the back it lies in, the stiff joint participates the least and gains little because the healthy joints above and below it work to achieve the movement. In this case, mobilisation and manipulation can 'exercise' and restore mobility to the stiff joint.

However, stretching exercises will nearly always be of benefit when a whole region of the spine is stiff, or when there is a stiffness problem at a joint which can be exercised in isolation, such as the hip, knee or shoulder.

Traction

Traction pulls the upper and lower halves of the body in opposite directions, either by machine or by hand. It is generally regarded as a gentle technique and is useful when the problem is more inflamed and painful.

Intermittent traction in gentle oscillation can relieve muscle spasm, possibly by pumping the tissues so that they flush away pain-producing waste metabolites (chemicals), and help reduce spasm. It seems to ease pressure and irritation of nerves, relieving conditions like sciatica.

Physiotherapists have traditionally used traction machines, but osteopaths and chiropractors often give traction manually. In either case, it can be applied continuously or intermittently. There are simple devices that can be hired or purchased to provide therapeutic neck traction in the home.

Shiatsu, acupressure and trigger points

In Japanese the word *shi* means finger and *atsu* means pressure. Shiatsu, also known as acupressure, is a specific form of massage in which fingers are pressed on particular, usually sensitive, points of the body to ease aches, pains, tension and fatigue.

Shiatsu is quite closely related to acupuncture, and involves similar ideas. It is said to restore health by unblocking obstructions in the meridian lines that connect the organs and allow the free flow of energy. Although the theory does not correlate with modern scientific views, the techniques still work well. Shiatsu is an effective method of relaxing muscles.

Western 'trigger points' mostly correspond with ancient Chinese acupressure points and are probably one and the same. These are irritable spots, sometimes quite deeply placed within a tight band of muscle or fascia, that can be felt as hard and painful when they are compressed. Unlike acupressure points, trigger points are not constant and pre-set but appear in response to an injury or pain and muscle tension. Chiropractors call trigger point therapy 'Nimmo technique', named after the chiropractor who practised and taught his version of trigger point massage.

Firm pressure or localised massage is applied to the shiatsu, acupressure or trigger point. The theory is speculative; however, it may be that the pressure stimulates a mild inflammatory response, causing the blood vessels to dilate. The increased blood flow washes away waste chemicals concentrated at the site. Like all massage, this reduces tenderness and pain, and therefore helps to relax the whole muscle. The technique may be effective because it focuses on the worst spot.

Shiatsu, acupressure and trigger point therapy belong broadly to the world of massage and are provided by massage therapists with specific training in the method.

Muscle energy technique

This goes by many names, such as contract–relax, hold–relax or proprioceptive neuromuscular facilitation (PNF).

Muscle energy techniques use the client's own muscular effort as the therapeutic force to relax spasm. This approach relaxes muscle by using two basic facts of muscle physiology. 'Post-isometric relaxation' means a muscle relaxes more after it has contracted. And, when muscle contracts, the antagonist, or opposite muscle, is obliged to relax in 'reciprocal inhibition'.

Many practitioners use simple versions of these techniques. A US osteopath, Fred Mitchell, developed them into a whole system of treatment that is safe, effective and painless. They can even be used as a self-treatment.

In these techniques, a joint restricted by injury is placed at the limit of its range. The client gently attempts to return it to normal while the practitioner resists movement. After the effort, the tight muscles relax a little, so the range is increased. The joint is then taken slightly further before the attempt is repeated.

For example, a stiff shoulder is treated by first raising it as far as possible. As the client attempts to pull it down, the therapist holds it still. The arm is then relaxed and moved slightly higher before the client again pulls down against resistance. After each effort, the arm can be elevated a bit further.

This approach is useful when stiffness and pain are due to muscular tightness. Sometimes it can relieve a joint stuck by muscle spasm. If the ligaments and joint capsule are the main problem, muscle energy techniques can relax surrounding muscle spasm before treatment is directed to the source of the trouble.

Cranial manual therapy

Cranial manual therapy, cranio-sacral therapy or cranial osteopathy is a therapy that still defies understanding. It is a method used mainly by osteopaths and chiropractors.

William Sutherland, a US osteopath, developed the therapy. He was convinced that the joints connecting the bones of the skull were designed to move. He felt minuscule rhythmic motions when he palpated his clients' heads. Trained practitioners sense that the whole head minutely widens and shortens, followed by a narrowing and elongation. The rate of this cranial or 'involuntary mechanism', between 3 and 12 cycles per minute, seems to be independent of the breathing and heart rate.

Practitioners working with the cranial method believe that this small movement can be influenced with the most gentle of all physical pressures. With hands resting on the client's head, they almost seem to use their mind alone to direct the treatment. To the client and onlookers, nothing may seem to happen. Cranial practitioners sense the same rhythm throughout the body and utilise it to treat all their patients' problems. Some combine this with conventional manual therapy.

The rhythm can be sensed by anyone with training. We do not understand it, nor do we understand the extent to which the minute movements that we sense occur in the client's body or the practitioner's mind. Although cranial practitioners use mechanical terminology to communicate their ideas, it is unclear whether the extremely small forces of treatment themselves physically move the tissues. Some other yet to be identified process might induce the changes necessary for recovery.

Dr Major Bertrand DeJarnette, a US chiropractor, developed sacro-occipital technique (SOT). He built on the ideas of Sutherland and developed techniques that enable trained SOT chiropractors to treat the body by the use of 'blocking'. They avoid manual force and place padded wedges under the resting body to achieve gravitationally assisted pressure or torque.

The range of problems suited to a cranial approach has not been clearly defined, nor has the efficacy of the method been proven. Supporters are usually osteopaths and chiropractors who treat the same problems as their colleagues. But they say it also helps young children with conditions that can extend to excessive crying, colic, glue ear, repeated infections, behavioural problems, hyperkinesia and learning difficulties, often said to be caused by the physical strains of a difficult birth.

Activator technique

Activator technique, used by chiropractors, is known for its use of a small hand-held spring-loaded device called an activator adjusting instrument (AAI). The activator delivers a small impact to the body when applied to the processes of the vertebrae and bony prominences of the pelvis. It was developed in the late 1960s by a US chiropractor, Alan Fuhr, and is thought to eliminate or reduce a subluxation.

Applied kinesiology

Applied kinesiology and a modified form, touch for health, uses a series of gentle muscle strength tests to detect mechanical disorders and other health problems. After applying the tests, the practitioner gives light fingertip massage to an appropriate tender point and re-tests the muscle to see that the problem has resolved.

George Goodheart, a US chiropractor, developed the idea in 1964. The client is shown how to put an arm or leg into a particular position and told to hold it steady. The practitioner then gently resists the stance, assessing its strength. The muscle testing checks 'circuits' to give a practitioner a picture of the client's state of health. The practitioner then tries to 'reset' the circuits which are found to be out of balance. Localised massage is given to 'pressure points', often some distance away from the weak muscle. Some of the concepts are similar to shiatsu and acupressure. The technique is thought to help by enhancing the flow of blood and lymph, and reducing stagnation and the build-up of poisons in the tissues.

In summary

So, there you are. I've described the common manual therapy techniques that you are likely to come across. Naturally, not all practitioners use all techniques and there is considerable variation within each profession. You might have to visit more than one practitioner to find the one that's right for you. We know that manual therapy as a whole works. Common sense, as well as scientific studies, tells us this. Millions of people walk away from their manual practitioner sensing profound improvement. There are vast numbers of happy and healthy converts to manual therapy. And there is no dispute about the numerous scientific studies which demonstrate that manual therapy gives fast recovery for mechanical problems in the spine and arms and legs.

CHAPTER SEVEN

WHO ARE THE MANUAL PRACTITIONERS?

- Bonesetters ■ Massage ■ Osteopathy
- Chiropractic ■ Manual medicine
- Manual physiotherapy

In this chapter I have divided manual therapy into the five broad professional groups that are found in Australia and New Zealand, as well as worldwide. They include, in their historical order, massage, osteopathy, chiropractic, manual medicine and manual physiotherapy. The section below on bonesetters places manual therapy in its historical context.

In the previous chapter I discussed several less mainstream manual approaches. These can be found under the subheading Massage (see p. 98). They include aromatherapy, reflexology, zone therapy, polarity balancing, Rolfing, postural integration and reiki.

Bonesetters

In Europe, manual therapy had an honourable history long before the development of osteopathy, chiropractic and physiotherapy.

Community manual therapists practised in England as long ago as the Middle Ages. Known as bonesetters, they flourished until well into the 20th century. In Europe they were called joint-setters and bone-knockers.

The name 'bonesetter' did not derive from setting broken

bones, but from the old name for realignment — the bones were 'set' into their correct position. Bonesetters probably treated the same problems as modern-day manual practitioners.

Methods were passed on from father to son as a family skill and occupation, in a similar manner to barber surgeons, midwives and other trades.

The most famous of all bonesetters was Sir Herbert Barker (1869–1950). In England, he was as well known as the best doctor of his time. His clients included royalty and nobility, members of parliament, famous actors and athletes. He was knighted for his work, although he was shunned by the medical profession because he had no medical qualifications and could not explain his methods.

As formal courses developed in manual treatment, osteopaths and chiropractors gradually replaced bonesetters. Sadly, much of the bonesetters' knowledge has been lost in the process.

Massage

(See also Chapter 6, Methods of Treatment)
Massage has been with us for an eternity; it is one of the oldest therapies known. It is among a few treatments that has a whole profession named after it. Since the dawn of recorded history, massage has been recognised as important to healing and comfort. Chinese physicians were massaging their clients 5000 years ago. In 430 BC the Greek physician Hippocrates wrote: 'It is necessary to rub the shoulder gently and smoothly following reduction of a dislocated shoulder', and 'Rubbing can loosen a joint that is too rigid and bind a joint that is too loose'.

The word itself is derived from the ancient Greek masso (I knead) and the Arabic mass (to press softly). Over the centuries it has become more sophisticated, with an increasing range of formally defined techniques, such as stroking, kneading, pressure, friction, vibration and percussion.

At the beginning of the 19th century, a Swede named Henrik Ling developed a theory that massage is a passive form of exercise. He created a system of treatment that combined massage and therapeutic exercise. Swedish movement treatment was developed in 1813, changing its name to Swedish massage as the system spread around the world. It became highly fashionable and spas which included his system sprang up throughout Europe.

In post-Victorian society, massage was associated with sweaty gyms, men with huge muscles and 'dubious' sexual practices. It smacked of Oriental culture and forbidden attention to physical pleasure.

Now that we are happier with the concepts of self-help and caring for our bodies, the therapeutic value of massage is once more being recognised. Massage is highly beneficial and often underrated.

Massage therapists, as they may be called, are becoming better educated, sometimes through government-funded courses. Full-time courses of up to three years' duration are available to those wishing to take up massage as an occupation. This has led to the formation of professional associations and better public awareness of their skills and services.

Many people have regular massages to counteract the relentless treadmill of work and personal pressure. It is good value for money and can deal effectively with many aches and pains.

Massage therapists often work from home, where their overheads are lower. They can also be found at sports and fitness centres, health resorts and beauty centres. In recent years, massage therapists have often been associated with physiotherapists, chiropractors, osteopaths and medical practitioners, sometimes in multi-disciplinary sports and musculoskeletal medicine practices.

Osteopathy

Nearly as old as modern medicine, osteopathy has been described as one of healthcare's best-kept secrets. It was established in 1876 by a US physician, Dr Andrew Taylor Still (1828–1917), as an alternative system of medicine.

Dr Still was a medical practitioner in the days when scientific medicine had hardly begun. There were no X-rays or antibiotics, medicines were still largely derived from herbs, and the idea that microscopic germs could cause diseases was only just becoming medical orthodoxy. (It is said that in 1869 Harvard University tried to institute written exams but the director of the medical school opposed the move on the grounds that many of the students could hardly write.)

Still's medical training proved to be of no help when he watched three of his sons die from meningitis. Spurred on by this harrowing tragedy he contemplated more effective methods of healing.

Observation led him to realise that many diseases were associated with identifiable changes in the soft tissues and joint mobility. The body seemed to have a better chance of combating disease and functioning well if these changes were somehow removed. It seemed as if healing was promoted by mechanical soundness. Dr Still successfully used the widely acknowledged principle that the body's natural tendency is to repair itself.

Dr Still taught himself palpation skills; he always carried a pocketful of small bones that he learnt to recognise, and he developed techniques for removing the mechanical disorders or 'osteopathic lesions' he could feel. He helped the body's natural powers of recovery to combat patients' sickness. Compared with orthodox medicine practised at the time, his methods were surprisingly effective on a wide variety of diseases. Mechanical and non-mechanical diseases, including infections, responded better if orthodox methods were supplemented or replaced with skilled 'hands on' methods.

The relative success and improvement on existing

methods led Still into a misconception. To him, it seemed that all diseases were caused by mechanical disorders, so he believed that osteopathy and manual treatment was nothing less than a complete system of medicine.

To osteopaths today, Dr Andrew Taylor Still is a remote but historically important figure, about as relevant as Lister or Hippocrates to conventional medicine. However, he made an enormous contribution to the whole of modern healthcare with his original and practical ideas. The development of osteopathy has had a major influence on manual therapy.

Osteopathy today

In the early 20th century, North American osteopathic courses kept pace with the development of medical education and tended to take about the same length of time to complete. It was quickly realised that there were many other causes of disease. Today, North American osteopathic training and treatment methods are similar to those of medicine.

As a result, the scope of osteopathy in North America is wider than elsewhere in the world. There are many osteopathic hospitals and they provide the complete range of health services, from paediatrician and pathologist to gynaecologist and surgeon. Patients may be quite unaware that their general practitioner is actually a Doctor of Osteopathy.

The main practical difference between osteopathic and medical doctors is in their use of manual therapy. An osteopathic physician is more conversant with manual skills and is prepared to use them when appropriate. However, there are some US osteopaths who exclusively practise manipulative osteopathy in the more narrowly defined field that we have come to accept.

Throughout the rest of the world, osteopathy is synonymous with osteopathic manual therapy. Although these practitioners do not offer a total health package, their training and the language they use is medically oriented, with treatment explained in accordance with modern medical theory. Osteopaths see themselves as complementary to medicine, not as an alternative. They offer people an additional treatment option in a well-defined range of conditions and care. However, although osteopathic manual therapy is now used on a relatively narrow range of health problems, osteopaths believe that manual therapy has a slightly wider role than that currently accepted by conventional medicine.

Osteopaths must be registered in Australia and New Zealand. University training is provided at five-year government-funded courses in Melbourne, Sydney and Auckland. Osteopathic treatment is covered under federal and state motor accident and workers' compensation schemes.

In Britain, osteopaths account for the largest group of manual practitioners and are often the first port of call for people wanting manual therapy. Their relationship with conventional medicine is good; Britain is the only country in the world where the government has registered osteopaths with the agreement and help of the medical profession. Osteopathic treatment under the National Health system is growing. Many colleges of osteopathy provide postgraduate training for physiotherapists and medical practitioners.

The rich and famous, as well as ordinary working people, attend osteopaths. The British Royal Family is well known for its interest in the area. Princess Anne has been patron of the British School of Osteopathy for many years, Prince Charles is patron of The General Osteopathic Council and the late Princess of Wales was president of the General Council and Register of Osteopaths. Prime ministers and presidents, distinguished sports people and celebrated actors have all attested to the manipulative expertise of osteopaths.

Chiropractic

Given that its history has been one of sustained medical opposition, it is quite remarkable that chiropractic is the most widely practised complementary therapy in the world. This says a great deal about the conviction, dedication and savvy of the chiropractic profession and the support given to it by the public.

Daniel David Palmer (1845–1913) founded chiropractic in 1895. Times were hard in Palmer's early adult life. Although he had no formal education, he was clearly intelligent and resourceful, if somewhat eccentric. He had already been a beekeeper, a grocer and a schoolmaster.

At the time, American country medicine in the post-Civil War years was far from satisfactory. There were few doctors and many of those were only half trained. A vast array of alternative healing methods had sprung up in response to ineffectual and sometimes dangerous medical treatments.

After considering several healing methods, Palmer decided to try magnetic healing. This was based on the theories of the first medical hypnotist, Mesmer, who transmitted 'magnetic healing forces' to the sick by repetitive hypnotic stroking.

Palmer claimed reasonable success over a period of 10 years, but he became increasingly fascinated by the idea of there being a single cause of human disease. He read about and continued to come into contact with a variety of healers. He would have been aware of and probably met Dr Andrew Taylor Still, who had already become famous practising osteopathy only a day's journey away. Some say that he did some training with Dr Still.

Palmer's answer to his quest for nature's secret of disease came to him in 1895 when he treated a caretaker in the building where he worked. Seventeen years earlier, the caretaker had lost his hearing after exerting himself at work and feeling something give in his back. Palmer examined him and found a painful vertebra in the upper part of the back. He had tried magnetic healing with no effect. So he gave an energetic push on the vertebra in question and shortly afterwards the man told him that he was beginning to hear again. With continued back treatment, the caretaker apparently gradually recovered his hearing.

Palmer thereafter examined the spines of all his clients, irrespective of the complaint. He found that treating what he thought to be displaced vertebra by manipulation frequently relieved symptoms in other parts of the body.

Palmer was convinced he could revolutionise the art of healing. Ironically, modern chiropractors have no satisfactory explanation for Palmer's original cure — manual therapy is not used to treat deafness.

Palmer developed and expanded his techniques, with many people flocking to his rooms for treatment. Within a year he began teaching a few interested clients and by 1903 his six-month long course had a dozen students.

He claimed that chiropractic was different from osteopathy in that he had developed the use of manipulation or joint cracking, which he called adjustment. This claim may be correct. There is no mention of manipulation in osteopathic history and Andrew Taylor Still certainly did not use the technique. In fact, Still openly criticised students of osteopathy who had learnt manipulation, presumably from the nearby Palmer School of Chiropractic.

While Daniel Palmer originated chiropractic, it was his son Bartlett Joshua Palmer (1881–1961) who gave the profession its momentum, growth and sometimes mixed reputation. Confident and domineering, he vigorously promoted the 'business of chiropractic'. Father and son often clashed over the development and direction of the profession.

While the discipline provided a good deal of benefit, its business orientation, educational standards and claims marred its reputation. Short courses in manipulation and marketing, leaving little space for growing medical knowledge, were commonly available. Chiropractic was a business opportunity and, to the irritation of medicine, flamboyant and misleading advertising was just a part of the business.

The expansion of chiropractic brought inevitable debates. American-trained Palmer school graduates were known as 'straights' for their purist insistence on the value of manipulation adjustments alone — often a more demanding treatment. Anything else was not chiropractic. The 'mixers' viewed themselves as more holistic and mixed their discipline with other forms of treatment such as massage, nutrition, homoeopathy and naturopathic remedies.

Chiropractic today

The chiropractic profession today bears little resemblance to those early beginnings. There has been enormous upgrading of educational standards in chiropractic colleges around the world. Today, students in Australia and New Zealand complete more hours of education than undergraduate physiotherapists and compare favourably with their medical and osteopathic colleagues.

In 1979 a New Zealand government inquiry conducted what must be the most thorough investigation ever made into chiropractic. The report provides a fascinating overview of chiropractic and its struggle to become an accepted profession. It is almost entirely favourable and repeatedly demonstrates weaknesses in the case of organised medicine against the chiropractic profession. The Commission of Inquiry found itself 'irresistibly and with complete unanimity drawn to the conclusion that modern chiropractic is a soundly-based and valuable branch of health care in a specialised area neglected by the medical profession'.

The number of chiropractors practising in the United States is greater than for the rest of the world combined. Public acceptance and government regulation there has largely outflanked medical opposition. Chiropractors are licensed in all states and workers' compensation plans pay for chiropractic treatment of industrial injuries. Commercial health and accident policies, and the private healthcare system, also provide for chiropractic treatment.

The growth of independent research has helped to legitimise chiropractic, as well as the role of manual therapies in general. Some, but not all, studies show that, for similar problems, manual treatment is more effective and less costly than medical treatment.

In Canada, there are numerous chiropractors, largely practising with the same rights and conditions as their counterparts in the United States.

In Australia, chiropractors are sometimes registered along with osteopaths under the same legislation. There are three university-based chiropractic programs in Melbourne, Sydney and Perth, all leading to Bachelor and Masters' degrees. Chiropractic is included under state and federal government Workers' Compensation Acts.

There are hundreds of chiropractors throughout Europe. In other countries, where chiropractors are more thinly spread, they are often the major providers of manual therapy.

Manual medicine

Manual medicine is the name given to the manual techniques practised by medical practitioners. This branch of medicine had no one starting point. Instead, it was an eclectic synthesis of techniques that worked for different enthusiasts. Medical historians point to a number of early medical manipulators who trained colleagues in the techniques of manual therapy.

Developing on the fringes of the medical establishment, manual medicine was stunted for years by opposition towards osteopathy and chiropractic. Its value has been recognised mainly in more recent decades, as prejudice against manual therapy has subsided.

The British Association of Manual Medicine, established in 1963, was the first medical association to have a special interest in manual therapy. There are now flourishing associations of manual medicine throughout the world and they provide regular, well-attended seminars. Some medical schools have introduced manual therapy as an option in their undergraduate courses.

Almost all the manual medicine skills were derived from osteopaths and chiropractors, and the early literature often acknowledges this debt.

Prominent among medical manipulators in England during the second half of the 20th century was James Cyriax of St Thomas' Hospital in London. He worked tirelessly to bring manual therapy to the attention of the medical profession. The London College of Osteopathic Medicine has been providing a one-year postgraduate course exclusively for medical practitioners since 1946. Its graduates have helped spread the tenets of manual medicine throughout the world. Dr Alan Stoddard, an osteopath and medical practitioner, has written several books on manual therapy which have been used as standard texts for courses in manual medicine for four decades.

In Europe, Dr Robert Maigne from Paris, and Drs Karel Lewit and Janda, both from Prague, have been prolific writers and teachers of manual medicine.

In North America, manual therapy was well supplied by osteopaths and chiropractors, so there was less demand for medical practitioners to develop manual skills. Only in more recent years has US mainstream medicine turned to support a manual approach.

Today, manual medicine techniques are taught at evening, weekend and other short seminars. Longer postgraduate diploma courses in musculoskeletal medicine teach manual skills as part of a package of examination and treatment methods, including injections, acupuncture, prescription of medication, psychological management and specialist referral. Few doctors exclusively practise manual therapy and the training tends to limit the range of manual techniques applied. Nevertheless, medical practitioners who practise manual therapy are often highly sought after by their patients and colleagues alike.

Manual physiotherapy

In the summer of 1894 there was much concern in the British medical and popular press about massage or 'medical rubbing' treatments which were practised in certain establishments disguised as nursing homes. In response, two young nurses decided to take positive action. In March 1895 they held examinations in the theory and practice of massage. Thus was started the profession of physiotherapy.

However, for the next 70 years physiotherapists largely ignored manual therapy. They worked as medical auxiliaries and were delegated work by doctors. Osteopaths and chiropractors were regarded as little better than charlatans performing rituals and dogma.

A few doctors realised that these 'lay practitioners' were offering a good deal more than trickery. Dr J. Mennell demonstrated manual therapy to physiotherapists at St Thomas' Hospital during the 1920s and 1930s. Dr James Cyriax, who was a great advocate of physiotherapists practising manual therapy, followed him to the same hospital.

In 1965 the Manipulative Therapists Association of Australia was the first group of physiotherapists to form a special interest group in manual therapy. During the late 1960s, Britain, New Zealand, Canada, the USA, South Africa, Holland, Norway, Sweden and Denmark all followed. In 1974 the International Federation of Manipulative Therapists was formed.

Many of the leading lights who have advanced the ideas of manual physiotherapy have written books on manual therapy. Geoff Maitland (Australia) and Freddy Kaltenborn (Sweden) both wrote books that have become standard texts for physiotherapy courses around the world. Physiotherapists Greg Grieve and Robin McKenzie have also written texts and contributed greatly to the profession in England and New Zealand.

Geoff Maitland, who works in Australia, published his first book *Vertebral Manipulation* in 1964; *Peripheral Manipulation* followed in 1970. His concept of oscillatory mobilisation to treat movement restrictions has had a profound influence and has been enthusiastically acclaimed by physiotherapists and medical practitioners alike. It has become the basis for teaching manual therapy to physiotherapists and doctors everywhere.

The number of physiotherapists practising manual therapy has grown enormously in recent years. After resisting the use of manual therapy for so long, they are now challenging chiropractors and osteopaths as major providers of manual therapy throughout the world.

CHAPTER EIGHT

DIFFERENCES BETWEEN THE BRANCHES

- Massage ■ Osteopathy ■ Chiropractic
- Manual medicine ■ Manual physiotherapy

Anyone considering using manual therapy is presented with a confusing variety of names. The same street could contain a masseur, an osteopath, a chiropractor, a manual physiotherapist and a doctor with manual therapy skills. You could be left with the uneasy feeling that there must be some profound differences between each one. Surely one group is better than another, or perhaps they are each good for different things?

It's important to keep the problem in perspective. The areas in common between the various manual schools are much more significant than are the differences. After all, there's a limit to the things that can be done with the hands when treating the same problems with the same purpose in mind. What's more, all branches of manual therapy, both complementary and orthodox, are learning techniques and skills from one another and converging. As hypothesis is replaced by evidence, the best aspects of each will undoubtedly continue to blend.

Some of the differences developed because each profession evolved in isolation from the others. Some differences were philosophical and dealt with competing explanations and alternative terms. These issues were important to each group because they concerned the ways in which practitioners pictured problems and applied treatment.

Some differences were due to government regulation. When registration was introduced, it occurred at different times and licensed different practices from community to community. Various countries allowed the forms of therapy to occupy different scopes of practice. In the United States, for instance, osteopaths have a similar scope and treat the same problems as medical practitioners, whereas in the rest of the world osteopathy is confined to manual therapy.

Where there was no government regulation, the differences between the various camps within a profession were often as great as the differences between the professions. The 'mixers' (those who mixed chiropractic with naturopathy, massage, homoeopathy, etc.) and the 'straights' (those chiropractors who only used manipulation) were at odds for years over which of their methods constituted true chiropractic.

This is the chapter where I will get into trouble with my own profession for explaining things as I see them, and with other manual professions for, let's face it, the same reasons! I have tried hard to be balanced and objective, but it is inevitable that my colleagues will not agree with everything I say. We all treat the same problems, so it is natural that each profession has its own spin on the differences, particularly behind the closed door of the consulting room.

Although the question is of significant interest to both patients and practitioners, in the public arena outside the consulting room a response to the question, 'What's the difference?' is often ducked or fudged. However, it remains one of the most frequently asked questions.

To the readers of this book, here are some answers. It is stressed that they are only opinions but they're given in the public arena, with common sense, and years of professional experience and input from colleagues from each of the manual professions. The views are more applicable within Australia and New Zealand but manual practitioners everywhere will recognise relevance in the comments. To manual practitioners who disagree and perceive bias and misrepresentation, I apologise — it is not intended. In a sense, describing the differences between the parties stimulates debate, and ultimately that will benefit everyone.

Fortunately for wounded pride and professional jealousy, there is little to suggest that one discipline is much more effective than another. In fact, the limited studies that have been carried out seem to indicate just the opposite — the result of treatment perhaps depends more on individual technical skills and experience than the particular profession a practitioner belongs to. Like painting or sculpture, manual therapy is very much a skill. Among manual practitioners, regardless of their profession, some show real aptitude for the job and are better at achieving results than others.

As research evidence replaces theories and dogma, manual practitioners are sharing more and more of each other's ideas, methods and knowledge. In the years to come, distinctions will undoubtedly continue to diminish.

Massage

A masseur's main focus is on relieving painful tension and stiffness in the muscles. It is also believed that massage can reduce the effects of emotional stress and anxiety, and restore a sense of 'wholeness'.

It's no surprise that massage is becoming increasingly well regarded by the public. Massage is a deeply relaxing and pleasurable experience. A demanding and tiring lifestyle harms well-being and increases the risk of stress-related conditions. The stress of modern living often results in muscular tension, for which massage can be the answer. Some medical practices have incorporated a masseur into their clinics to assist with their patients' physical and emotional health.

The differences between massage and the other manual therapies are not nearly as great as may be thought. A masseur's case history is usually more straightforward, as there are fewer things to go wrong in the muscles. Massage concentrates on the overlying covering of muscles that can be grasped, squeezed and kneaded directly, with relatively little movement of the joints and body framework. Massage therefore helps most when pain and muscular tension reside in the overlying, accessible layers of muscles; whereas reaching the deep soft tissues (ligaments, joint capsule and disc) requires movement techniques such as stretching, mobilisation and manipulation.

Massage therapists say that humane, caring massage is important for both the body and the mind. They see a relationship between physical sensations of muscular pain and tension, and mental suffering, conflict and anxiety. They say: 'Relax the body and the mind will follow'. Relaxing the physical body harmonises conscious thought and gives balance and clarity to the daily life we lead. In times of stress, massage helps us to see our way forward more clearly.

Not surprisingly, a massage treatment takes the longest of all the manual therapies. The shortest massage session is 30 minutes, but a masseur may give 45 minutes, one hour or longer depending on the purpose of the massage. A good massage is highly beneficial and good value, and often solves a client's muscular and emotional tension.

For many mechanical problems, massage provides all that is needed for remedy. A competent masseur will tell you if a medical opinion or advice from another manual practitioner should be sought.

Masseurs, of course, focus on massage, which tends to give them a particular area of knowledge and skills. Within the profession, some are purists, many are eclectic. Remedial massage, relaxation massage, sports massage, acupressure, shiatsu, aromatherapy, reflexology, polarity therapy and Rolfing are just some of the treatments given by a masseur.

(Refer to Chapter 6 for explanations on several of the above techniques.)

Massage is back in favour; the therapy suits our busy times and it is often the way to go.

Osteopathy

A long appointment, gentle treatment, a few visits per problem and treatment on an 'as needs' basis are the hallmarks of osteopathy. An osteopath's main focus is on the soft tissues that give rise to symptoms.

Osteopaths claim that their approach is the most effective of the manual therapies. They suggest that you should consider consulting an osteopath for a difficult, longstanding or recurring problem, or a problem that has stopped progressing with other methods.

Osteopaths, like chiropractors, use manual therapy for a slightly wider range of disorders than manual physiotherapists and medical practitioners; they treat functional problems. However, unlike chiropractors, who tend to rely more extensively on X-rays, osteopaths will only request X-rays to screen for pathological changes in the bones, as in conventional medicine, and are not so interested in the alignment of the vertebrae.

The initial consultation takes about 30 minutes. After that, most treatment sessions take from 20 to 30 minutes. Practitioners claim that the length of an osteopathic treatment is one reason for its success. Several minutes of any visit is spent on discussing and reviewing symptoms, re-examination, case reports and patient changeover, all of which eats into the 'hands on' treatment time. Therefore, a small increase in contact time can greatly increase the effectiveness of the overall treatment. For example, a 20-minute appointment might allow 15 or 16 minutes of actual treatment, whereas a 10-minute appointment provides only five or six minutes of 'hands on' treatment.

Doubling the appointment time might give three times the treatment.

Although it was the first of the modern manual professions, osteopathy can appear to be a judicious combination of massage and chiropractic. A typical treatment might be divided into three stages. The session could begin with massage to relax the overlying muscles. A significant part of each appointment is spent on this component. Muscle energy and spontaneous release techniques can be used here to help reduce muscle spasm. Next, articulation and mobilisation techniques might further free up tight tissues, so that movement begins to be restored. Finally, mobilisation with impulse (manipulation) can release stuck joints and loosen the deep, most inaccessible tissues.

Patients find this graded sequence of steps comfortable and effective. It is one of osteopathy's strengths and another reason why those who try osteopathy stay with it. If manipulation is needed, it is gentle and easily achieved. Patients comment that they 'prefer not to be manipulated cold'; they recognise that manipulation without adequate preparation can be stressful and sometimes alarming.

Osteopaths claim that their approach provides effective outcomes with few visits. A survey in Britain indicated that one in six osteopathic appointments are patients consulting an osteopath for the first time. Four to six sessions are thought to be a common number of visits.

Osteopathic treatment is provided on an 'as needs' basis; the profession's reputation is built on discharging patients. Osteopaths claim that their long appointment time and treatment methods make reliance on maintenance visits less necessary. Each case is assessed individually. Maintenance treatment might be recommended for some unresolved problems or recurring symptoms, such as might be the case in a longstanding or widespread problems, or when persistent pain and stiffness is associated with conditions like arthritis.

Some osteopaths, like some chiropractors, manual physiotherapists and doctors, don't rely on manipulation techniques to the same extent as others. They may use other methods such as muscle energy, spontaneous release and cranial osteopathy. Their particular style will have been moulded by the increased choice of techniques, the results they achieve with them, their training methods, their personal aptitude and confidence, their consideration of the risk or the occasional experience of adverse effects from manipulation.

An osteopathic approach is not unique to osteopaths. Some practitioners are chiropractors or physiotherapists in name but have an osteopathic approach to treatment. To get some idea when seeking out a manual practitioner, ask about the length of their appointments. A longer appointment might indicate more hands-on time and perhaps a more osteopathic style. If other treatment is not providing the answers for you, osteopathic manual therapy is worth seeking out.

Chiropractic

Treatment by adjustment, X-ray examination, maintenance visits, marketing and a different vocabulary are some of the hallmarks of chiropractic. A chiropractor tends to focus on the bones.

Chiropractors are extremely proud of their history and their successful battle against the odds; they have a passionate attachment to their ideas and methods. They took great satisfaction when a 1979 New Zealand government report into chiropractic said: 'Chiropractors are the only health practitioners who are necessarily equipped by their education and training to carry out spinal manual therapy'.

Marketing has been kind to chiropractic; it has greatly helped to raise public awareness and numbers in the profession. Before government regulation limited advertising, chiropractors grew to become the largest and best known complementary healthcare profession in the world. Their clinics are now often seen on busy roads and street corners where they can be easily found when needed.

A chiropractor is more likely to request an X-ray examination. A US-trained chiropractor might regard it as essential and keep the equipment on his or her premises. In diagnosis, X-rays reveal bone pathology and reasons to modify or avoid manipulative treatment. Many chiropractors claim that the alignment of the bones also helps locate a subluxation and indicate the type and direction of adjustment they should apply.

Chiropractors call their treatment techniques 'adjustments'. An adjustment varies between the gentle oscillation of a joint, similar to a physiotherapist's mobilisation, to the more familiar joint cracking that manipulation is known for. There is less emphasis on more time-consuming massage and articulation. This is regarded as an advantage as it makes the approach more specific and focused on the core of the problem, the vertebral subluxation (mechanical disorder).

Although the length of an appointment varies, chiropractors generally allow about the same time as a medical practitioner. The initial consultation takes about 30 minutes, whereas follow-up treatments usually take 10 to 15 minutes. The average patient makes about 12 visits to a chiropractor for a particular problem.

Probably influenced by the same factors that have affected other manual practitioners, some chiropractors have drifted away from joint-cracking techniques. They may use the Activator technique or Sacro-occipital technique (SOT). (See Chapter 6, Activator technique and Cranial manual therapy.)

Patients are encouraged to attend maintenance treatment or check-ups, making regular visits similar to a dentist so that any future problem might be avoided. This idea arose when it was realised that many mechanical disorders had a pre-existing underlying problem. There might be scar tissue from an earlier injury, arthritic changes, joint disease, postural strain or chronic joint stiffness. The pre-existing condition causes symptoms to occur at lower levels of physical stress than the body would otherwise tolerate, and the body to recover more slowly. Maintenance visits are thought to help contain the pre-existing problem and prevent the pain returning.

Chiropractors' everyday vocabulary can differ from other manual practitioners. The modern chiropractic profession, which explains mechanical problems in accordance with modern medical theory, is still very young. There are many established and skilled chiropractors who belong to the old 'bone out of place' school. Their diagnoses and waiting room pamphlets tend to emphasise the bones and nerves. Ill health is said to be due to bone misalignments interfering with the nerves. Although the explanations may be different to those of other manual practitioners, they do not alter the quality of chiropractic care.

Over the last 25 years, chiropractic education, research and professional standards have progressed beyond recognition. Chiropractors' enthusiasm and belief in themselves is irresistible. Their treatment is widely accepted by the community; they are the most visible and best known providers of manual therapy, and are often the first port of call.

Manual medicine

Manual medicine is the name given to manual therapy practised by medical practitioners. Despite its different name, manual medicine has far more in common with the other manual professions. In its early days, manual medicine learnt from osteopathy and chiropractic. It is now drifting away from manipulation techniques towards mobilisation and muscle energy techniques. These methods are easier to learn and apply, and quite often are just as effective.

Doctors have had a surprisingly large impact on manual therapy. Despite the reservations of organised medicine about osteopathy and chiropractic, many of the world's leading writers and researchers on manual therapy have been medically trained.

There are few doctors who practise manual medicine exclusively. Most are general practitioners with an interest in using manual techniques in their practice. There are some advantages: they have a broad range of medical skills, they inspire confidence in their diagnosis and they are covered by government-funded health services.

In a general practice setting, manual doctors expect that their contact time will be about 15 minutes. Their methods centre on mobilisation and muscle energy techniques, with less emphasis on soft tissue massage. Nevertheless, there are no 'quickie' manual therapy appointments and the length of a session is usually longer than in general practice.

Some medical practitioners specialise in the practice of 'musculoskeletal medicine'. Previously called manual medicine and physical medicine, this discipline deals with disorders of the musculoskeletal system. It covers conditions that fall between the areas of help provided by a general practitioner and other specialties such as rheumatology, orthopaedic surgery and rehabilitation medicine. Musculoskeletal physicians combine manual therapy with injections, acupuncture, prescription of medication, psychological management and specialist referral.

Some manual professions have expressed concern that doctors practising manual therapy are in some way treading on their toes and taking work away from them. In fact, the reverse is more likely. Medical practitioners who practise manual therapy tend to be more aware of the indications for specialised manual skills and will often refer the patient to a manual physiotherapist, chiropractor or osteopath. Patients and manual practitioners alike benefit from the increased medical understanding of manual therapy.

Manual physiotherapy

Manual physiotherapists have a preference for the techniques of mobilisation over manipulation. They also use electrotherapy (such as ultrasound or interferential therapy), heat packs, supportive braces and exercises, and maintain close relations with the medical profession. A physiotherapist focuses on the joint associated with a mechanical problem.

Physiotherapists are introduced to manual therapy as undergraduates and learn the discipline in depth at postgraduate courses. These can extend from a series of weekend courses to a one-year full-time or two years part-time postgraduate diploma qualification.

Mobilisation techniques are central to their treatment methods and are greatly preferred to manipulation. Mobilisation uses rhythmic oscillations to restore movement to a joint. It is seen as a safe and effective way of helping joints, whereas manipulation is more difficult, takes longer to learn and incurs a slight risk.

Manual physiotherapists tend to avoid treating functional

disorders of the viscera, as criticised by conventional medicine. The more select range of conditions that doctors have seen fit to refer to them has moulded their experience.

Manual physiotherapists' appointments usually provide for four clients per hour, but this does not necessarily mean that each appointment is 15 minutes long. Because they often use equipment, they tend to set patients up and move on to others so they are effectively caring for a group of people at any one time. This can be a more efficient use of resources, with clients spending up to an hour in treatment. However, the manual therapy component naturally requires one-to-one contact.

Undergraduate training emphasises therapeutic exercise. This can help treat injuries between consultations, encourage recovery, provide ways in which people can treat minor recurrences themselves, reduce dependence on treatment and generally maintain health. Water exercise (hydrotherapy) has been developed to increase strength and mobility with the least strain and discomfort to the body.

Physiotherapists can use traction, ultrasound and other types of electrotherapy equipment. Collars, corsets, braces and other aids may be prescribed to give immediate protection and support. These can be useful in acute conditions that might be too delicate for manual treatment. For example, a soft neck collar can protect and support a painful whiplash injury in the early days after a motor accident. A knee brace gives strength and protection to many knee injuries, while allowing continued use of the knee.

Physiotherapy maintains close relations with medicine and it is argued that this benefits patients. It is claimed that they are more likely to recognise their limitations and refer clients for tests, medical treatment or specialist review.

Manual physiotherapy has added several ideas to the field of manual therapy, including 'neural stretching'. These stretches are used when there is pain along the course of a nerve in the arm or leg. It is thought to help pain by loosening adhesions between the nerve and the tissue it passes through.

Perhaps the most valuable development of physiotherapy has been the mobilisation techniques. Developed by Australian physiotherapist Geoff Maitland, mobilisations are push-and-release oscillatory pressures, commonly given with the thumbs and used to loosen stiff joints. They are liked because they are gentle and easy to learn and help the large majority of cases suited to manual treatment.

Although manual physiotherapy is the new kid on the manual therapy block, it has become a major player in recent decades.

When considering a visit to a manual practitioner, don't tear your hair out about which profession you should choose. It's much more important that you are happy with the individual practitioner than the profession they belong to. Every practitioner seems to attract his or her adherents. Have you ever noticed how many of your friends and work colleagues say: 'You must go to my person. There's no one better.' It's like the hairdresser, clothing or fruit shop that you favour because it suits your needs. Almost everybody seems to go to the best person in the business! And, if you're not happy, it's time to move on.

For further help on choosing a practitioner with qualities that meet your needs see Chapter 18, Finding your manual practitioner.

CHAPTER NINE

DEBATES ABOUT MANUAL THERAPY

- Unproven science ■ Education
- Claims ■ The placebo effect
- Dangers ■ Unprofessional behaviour
- X-rays ■ The current medical attitude

There has been a long history of official medical antagonism towards osteopaths, chiropractors and masseurs. This chapter explains the root causes of the opposition, what the remaining concerns are and why resistance has lessened but not yet disappeared.

More and more, attitudes are changing; there is an increasing coming together of the parties. But it takes time for misconceptions and prejudices to subside and newer approaches to become accepted. Even now, the public still senses that consulting an osteopath, chiropractor or masseur might not be generally approved and there is a common tendency not to mention their visit when patients consult their medical practitioner.

In the past, the medical profession opposed manual practitioners for their unproven treatment methods, educational standards, claims and beliefs, unprofessional behaviour and use of a treatment method that some said was dangerous.

Undoubtedly, some of the censure was accurate and appropriate; it has led to change. Some was wide of the mark, only serving to delay acceptance of a highly effective and safe form of treatment.

Osteopathy had an easier passage than chiropractic.

Osteopaths in the United States put their house in order early in the 20th century when organised medicine was less opposed. This has allowed them the opportunity to mature as a profession. Chiropractors were slower off the mark, their actions drawing more criticism. By the time they sought regulation, the other professions had ganged up against them.

Orthodox reservations are diminishing. Medicine is now largely embracing and accepting the value of manual therapy, but it continues to keep at arm's length what it still regards as myths and dogma.

Unproven science

It was suggested that manual therapy was based on untested theories and on a single unproven treatment method.

It is true there are many occasions where we do not know exactly how and why manual therapy works. There has been a shortage of scientific investigation into back problems. Good research is expensive and, until recent times, the manual professions have not had the resources to fund complex clinical trials using funded, professional research staff.

Research is most important, but the fact that manual therapy is not precisely explained and proven does not mean that treatment is ineffective. Theories are only attempts to explain results. The history of medicine is littered with examples of theories that did not fit into the orthodox framework, from the idea of blood circulating around the body to Lister's use of antiseptics during surgery. A large proportion of medical treatments as we know them today have developed from the results of practical experience rather than scientific research. Aspirin, made from willow tree bark, has been used to relieve pain and reduce inflammation for centuries before people knew what it was and how it worked.

Of course, some research has taken place. Most

researchers have investigated the basic question of whether manual therapy works, and compared it with other treatments such as heat, corsets, medication or a placebo. There are studies with ambiguous results, but generally when manual therapy is compared with other methods it is demonstrated that manual treatment provides some of the quickest relief from pain that is musculoskeletal in origin.

One Australian study on migraine in the 1970s established that manual therapy was an effective treatment. Although still debated today, until this result was published most orthodox authorities believed that a patient who had relief from manual therapy was not suffering from genuine migraine but some other type of headache. (See Chapter 12, Migraine.)

The small amount of research carried out has only just scratched the surface. Until there is greater scientific understanding, both doubters and believers can continue to stand their ground.

Education

Some critics have claimed that the education of osteopaths (apart from US-trained osteopaths) and chiropractors was not equivalent to that of a medical practitioner. It was therefore said to be insufficient to safeguard the public.

This logic does not stand up to analysis. The training of doctors takes longer only because it is broader. Manual practitioners do not attempt to manage the entire spectrum of health problems, as do medical practitioners. Manual therapy is a specialised treatment, similar to dentistry, optometry or podiatry, and appropriate only to certain specific conditions.

In Australia and New Zealand, osteopathic and chiropractic courses are five years' duration, and manual physio-therapists do four years of undergraduate training followed by one year of postgraduate study.

There are growing numbers of chiropractors, osteopaths and physiotherapists undertaking doctoral research. They present their work in scientific forums and contribute to the debates on improving healthcare. The truth is that where government regulation has taken place, osteopaths and chiropractors, as well as manual physiotherapists, are well educated, highly skilled and safe. The public is adequately protected against incompetence.

Claims

In their early days, both osteopathy and chiropractic claimed to be a total healthcare system. Every disorder, whether pneumonia, appendicitis or backache, was treated by the osteopath or chiropractor. However, these misconceptions have largely been corrected and neither profession would claim to manage every health problem by using manual therapy.

It is no longer possible to find fault on these grounds, so the criticism has changed. Now it is said that manual medicine practitioners and manual physiotherapists, the two most orthodox branches, know their limitations, but osteopaths and chiropractors do not. A small area of disagreement remains.

It is true that conventional medicine has resisted the idea of mechanical disorders causing functional disturbances in the viscera. (See Chapter 4, Functional disorders.) The back may not be considered in people with symptoms referred to the abdomen and chest. Medical practitioners come to manual therapy after a traditional medical education and tend to be more cautious. They prefer to restrict themselves to obvious spine, joint and muscle problems.

However, osteopaths and chiropractors believe that this reservation is unwarranted. They have over a century of practice and successful treatment to support their claims. They believe that as the research evidence unfolds a slightly wider role for manual therapy will become apparent.

The placebo effect

A placebo effect occurs when a person's condition improves while they have been taking medicine which is of no physiological value. A doctor might prescribe a placebo if symptoms, such as fatigue, ill-defined digestive disorders or stress, are not caused by an illness that requires specific medication. The benefit gained by taking the placebo occurs because the person taking it believes that it will help. It is a well-recognised phenomenon in medicine and all good researchers take it into account.

Some early opponents of manual therapy claimed that symptom recovery was entirely due to the placebo effect and that manual therapy had no value at all. If this were really so, and it is not, it would mean that manual practitioners had made an enormous contribution to humanity. They could cure problems by the 'laying on of hands' when conventional treatment had already failed in the same case!

It is true, however, that the placebo effect is particularly powerful in the treatment of mechanical disorders where stress and anxiety intensify muscular tension and pain. The laying on of hands and such things as taking the time to listen and understand the problems, confidence, skill, gentleness and reassurance all help to promote recovery by relieving fears and emotional muscular tension. We manual practitioners are trained to be very good at these things.

The attitudes of those who receive manual therapy appear to be overwhelmingly positive. With few exceptions, patients become satisfied clients who do not hesitate to recommend manual services to their ailing friends and relatives.

Dangers

In the past, it was said that manual practitioners treated people who desperately needed medical treatment and that they caused terrible injuries due to the vigour of their attentions.

The dangers of manual therapy have been greatly overstated by those with a vested interest in undermining it, or who are ignorant of the realities. Hearsay abounds with stories of those who were maimed or died from manipulation. It is quite another matter to verify the stories, for accidents and poor judgement, which do occur, are very rare. The risks of manipulation are very low in skilled hands.

Manipulative treatment is predominantly gentle, comfortable and relaxing. Patients mostly find it pleasant and easy to accept. Almost all treatments have potentially hazardous effects and something can go wrong despite every reasonable precaution being taken. This is just as true of medicine and surgery, where the risks can be substantial and the consequences severe.

Occasionally, a manual technique can injure the structure it was designed to help. In these cases, the problem is usually mild and temporary. Manipulation (joint cracking) techniques are slightly more demanding, and statistics show that they carry greater risk. Of the serious complications, 80 per cent arise in the neck. Most of these are due to the technique injuring blood vessels around the spinal cord and supplying the brain.

There is no one professional group who is more responsible for serious complications. Manual doctors and musculoskeletal physiotherapists, as well as osteopaths and chiropractors, all seem to have their share. If the cost of professional indemnity malpractice insurance is any guide, as described in the introduction, it confirms that manual therapy is low risk when compared with other healthcare modalities. Premiums are low and malpractice claims against manual practitioners are few.

Studies of serious complications arising from manual therapy vary quite widely. The median figures suggest that one occurs in about 100 000 manipulations. Perhaps one out of two or three manual practitioners will have one serious complication during their career. By medical standards this is an extraordinary low rate. It would still be low even if complications were to occur, as some suggest, more frequently than is reported in the literature.

Students are taught to understand the risks and types of complication. With greater professional awareness of the risks of neck manipulation it is likely that improved practice will lead to further reductions in the already low rate of complications.

A past leader in orthopaedic medicine, Dr James Cyriax, has said that it is less harmful to manipulate than not to manipulate. While the dangers of treatment are slight, the failure to intervene could leave the patient trapped in chronic pain and insidiously progressive disability, and vulnerable to the greater risks of medicine and surgery. The truth is that manual therapy in skilled hands is remarkably safe and complications are the exception.

Unprofessional behaviour

There is no doubt that some manual practitioners have behaved less professionally than their medical colleagues. In the past, pamphlets and publicity material often contained misleading and untrue assertions. For example, it was said that treating the spine could help medical problems such as leukaemia, diabetes, blood pressure, hernia and acne. Flamboyant advertising, more appropriate to selling a packet of cornflakes, was commonplace. There were even threats of ill health unless you attended for treatment.

The problem is disappearing, particularly in countries where government regulation has been put in place. However, despite the new sense of responsibility, manual therapists as a whole tend to be brought into disrepute by their history and the continued unprofessional activities of a few. Some simplistic promotional material and 'Confidential Patient Reports' would be quite laughable if not for the fact that the public take them seriously.

In the past, advertising has been particularly irritating to mainstream medicine. Rules are now becoming increasingly relaxed to allow all practitioners, including medical practitioners, to advertise their special interests and skills. However, except for these regulated notices, advertising is still regarded in most countries as self-promotion and unethical.

In the United States, this issue is viewed a little differently. There, advertising is commonplace, even though it may be judged as objectionable by standards in other countries.

Many chiropractors around the world have trained in the United States and have come into contact with this type of promotion. They have learnt the commercial benefits and tend to be more extroverted as advertisers in comparison with other manual practitioners. Most manual therapy professions now vigorously police the advertising of their members.

Some advertising still exists and people should be wary of claims. Practitioners who claim to relieve a wide variety of medical diseases should be avoided, since they demonstrate ignorance that could translate into dangerous treatment.

You should beware of therapists who encourage patients to consult them before seeing a medical practitioner for any health problem at all. A manual practitioner can be consulted after the failure of conventional treatment or when it is fairly obvious that the problem relates to the musculoskeletal system. After all, the great majority of sick people need medical treatment.

Unnecessarily prolonged treatment without improvement is clear evidence of unprofessional behaviour. It can be a major problem in countries where third party insurers pay for treatment of industrial and motor accident injuries. A person might enjoy attending for a therapy they do not pay for and the practitioner might be happy to continue collecting a fee without the client improving. Some improvement should be apparent in most cases within three or four visits. There should be sound reasons for continuing treatment without clear progress. If satisfactory reasons are not given, you should discontinue treatment and seek another opinion.

X-rays

There is growing doubt about the value of routine X-ray examination to investigate those receiving manual therapy. The relationship between pain and many bony abnormalities seen on X-ray is much more limited than was once thought. It appears that the X-ray appearance of congenital (birth) bone anomalies, mild to moderate scoliosis (curvature), disc degeneration, spondylosis (spinal degeneration) and osteoarthritis, to name a few, have little correlation with pain.

Moreover, most chiropractors now say there is no credible evidence that vertebral misalignments seen on X-ray are the painful mechanical disorders that they treat. Further, there is no justification for routine X-ray examination to assess for bony misalignments.

Medicine has been unsure about how to react to routine

X-rays of every person receiving manual therapy. On the one hand, X-rays are obviously valuable and it is prudent and responsible to assess the strength of bones having leverage and force put through them. On the other hand, X-rays, and indeed any test, should not be ordered indiscriminately without reference to the likely diagnostic yield, the risks and the cost.

Historically, chiropractors thought that the misalignments they saw on X-ray were the mechanical disorders they treated, so they took X-rays of every client. As the misalignment theory came under question for many reasons, but primarily because the X-ray data did not support it, there was debate about whether the need for X-rays related more to misalignments or to medical diseases. The emphasis of chiropractic X-ray examination is now placed on the search for medical disease in the bones; the profession's view is becoming more aligned with other health professions. Although the reasons for taking X-rays have changed, some chiropractors still request them for each new client.

Osteopaths, manual doctors and manual physiotherapists refer patients for X-ray examination less frequently. They request them only when the procedure is likely to add useful medical information that is unavailable by other means. There is no evidence to show that this convention makes their therapy any less safe.

You are recommended to keep and look after your own X-ray films, together with a copy of the report. Your home is the best place to store your X-rays. If there is no report in the X-ray envelope, ask for a copy. Seeking a second opinion and treatment is common practice with musculoskeletal problems, so it is sensible to ask your practitioner for the X-rays or at least a copy of the report.

The current medical attitude

These days the work of manual practitioners is generally accepted by orthodox medicine. After all, we speak the same language and there is no great sense of mysticism or profoundly opposing views. The disputes are no more serious than those between surgeons arguing the merits of various operations or researchers hypothesising in their field of science.

In many ways, the relationship between orthodox medicine and manual therapists is harmonious. Increasing numbers of medical practitioners recommend their patients consult a manual practitioner, be they a masseur, manual physiotherapist, chiropractor or osteopath. A small but growing number of medical practitioners have incorporated a manual practitioner into their group practice. They like to know they can offer a solution to some of their patients' intractable problems.

Professional medical bodies, often regarded as the most conservative and the last to accept new ideas, are starting to recommend a positive approach towards complementary health practitioners who meet defined levels of competence. Professional standards, research, government-funded training, registration, medical interest and a growing understanding of manual therapy have all contributed to the change of attitude.

It remains true, however, that the majority of medical practitioners and specialists have a limited understanding of manual therapy. More research needs to be carried out to define precisely which cases will benefit from manual therapy. There is insufficient training for medical practitioners to identify appropriate cases to refer to manual practitioners, and even less training in the practice of manual therapy. Quite often manual therapy is not recommended when it should be, and doctors may not realise that some functional disorders have mechanical origins. Even today the great majority of patients who come to a manual practitioner do so on their own initiative or on the advice of friends.

It is hard to blame the medical profession for its caution. Manual therapy has been brought into disrepute by unsubstantiated claims, poor standards of training, the wide range of conditions treated and unprofessional behaviour. The result is that most medical schools do not teach students about the role of manual therapy, and medical education relating to the biomechanics and neurophysiology of the spine remains limited.

Without proof, mainstream medicine does not accept the claim that a small group of back problems can affect the organs and be treated by mechanical means, but the gap between the parties is narrowing. Doctors are learning more about manual therapy and the standards of care, which can only be of benefit to the public.

PART TWO
A GUIDE TO SYMPTOMS AND WHAT THEY MIGHT MEAN

CHAPTER TEN

GENERAL MECHANICAL DISORDERS

- Cracking joints ■ Growing pains
- Muscle spasm (hypertonia)
- Osteoarthritis ■ Rheumatism
- Soft tissue injury ■ Subluxation

Cracking joints

Several noises may be both heard and felt in the joints of the back, arms and legs during joint movement. Mostly they are temporary and harmless — they do not indicate a problem and are considered to be a normal part of joint behaviour. If a joint is persistently noisy or accompanied by pain and stiffness then advice should be sought. Abnormal tension in the muscles that work the joint is the most common cause of noisy joints. Manual therapy is usually helpful.

Types

Cavitation is the sharp sound of joint manipulation. (See Chapter 6, The crack.) The noise is caused by the collapse of a gas bubble formed within the joint after the two halves are separated. It may be carried out intentionally by a manual practitioner or by those who like to crack their own fingers; sometimes it occurs inadvertently. Inadvertent cracking usually has little significance and does not require advice unless it is persistent or accompanied by pain or stiffness.

Crepitation is a sandpaper-like noise that can sometimes be felt and heard during movement, such as when the head is turned left and right or in the knees when squatting. It is associated with early wear of the joint cartilage. The noise becomes more noticeable when the sliding surfaces are compressed by muscular tension. The thin film of lubricating synovial fluid, which separates the two surfaces, is squeezed out so that minor surface irregularities are felt as a sandpaper-like sensation.

Try turning your head left and right when you're tired; you may notice a gritty, sandpaper-like feeling This sensation reduces after rest, massage or stretching exercises relax the tense muscles and allow the fluid film to recover.

Fine crepitation changes to coarse crepitation as cartilage becomes more worn. When cartilage becomes worn down completely and bone rubs on bone, there is a marked, almost jumping, roughness.

A *joint-tracking* click is the repeated pop or catching sensation at a certain point of movement. It is a common phenomenon and can be experienced in any joint, such as the knee, shoulder, elbow, neck or back. It may be the result of excessive tone in one of the muscles working the joint. The extra tension is unsynchronised with the other muscles that move the joint and prevents the sliding surfaces from changing their point of contact in a continuous and smooth manner. A click occurs at a point of sudden slippage.

A *snapping* tendon occurs when a tendon suddenly slips over a bony prominence. It mainly occurs at mobile joints like the hip and shoulder, and is again probably due to excessive tension in the muscle attached to the tendon. A persistent snapping tendon can become painful.

Treatment

Many joint sounds are transient and will resolve themselves without treatment. Simply bending and straightening the joint doing some exercises or self-massage will help reduce tension in the tight muscle and stop the noisy trouble.

If it is persistent or associated with pain or stiffness, most cases can be resolved with manual therapy. Treatment may include relaxing tight muscles, freeing up any underlying joint stiffness and exercising which can be done at home.

Growing pains

Growing pains, those vague aches and pains that occur in the limbs of children aged between 8 and 14, is a controversial subject. Medical texts largely avoid and omit the condition, while family health encyclopedias that cater for the community tend to include it. Most of us can remember as a youngster going to bed and being told that an aching joint is only due to 'growing pains'. As a parent it is an easy answer and puts to rest what appears to be a minor complaint at the end of a busy day.

Growing pains mostly occur at night. They mainly affect the legs and arms, and seem to follow activity and sport. Although the cause of growing pains is unknown, they do not appear to be related to bones or to the process of bone growth. An explanation might lie in a growing child's lanky proportions. Fast-growing children have long bones before their scrawny muscles thicken out to give their joints strength and protection. At this stage the muscles and joints may not be able to withstand the strains that the longer leverages place on them as they run round the schoolyard and play sport. When more mature, thicker and stronger proportions develop, growing pains seem to subside. So growing pains are perhaps mild strains of the muscles and joints, and are not a problem of the bones. This explains why growing pains respond so well to manual therapy.

Muscle spasm (hypertonia)

Spasm is sustained involuntary contraction of muscle, often caused by strong pain in a neighbouring structure such as a fractured bone or dislocated joint. Hypertonia is a less intense contraction than spasm, usually seen in less painful conditions. It is the normal response in the mechanical disorders we treat. Muscle hypertonia accompanies joint sprain, disc prolapse, fatigue, emotional stress, poor posture and sprain of the muscle itself. Its purpose is to splint an injury and protect it from further damage. Having said that, the popular term for both types of involuntary muscle contraction is spasm and this is the word that I will use.

One of the problems of muscle spasm is that the tension itself is often painful. The tightness limits the free flow of blood, reduces clearance of waste chemicals and the supply of fresh oxygen. The excess waste chemicals and lack of oxygen is painful and sets up the vicious circle of 'pain–spasm–pain', causing the problem to remain.

Treatment

Although treatment is usually directed at the cause of the spasm, reducing the muscle spasm itself is a necessary first step. This may include applying a cold or hot pack, or alternating 10 minutes hot, followed by 10 minutes cold. Together they help to relax the spasm, increase the blood flow and flush away waste chemicals.

Analgesic medication (pain-killers) helps to reduce pain and can interrupt the pain–spasm–pain cycle by relaxing the muscles.

Manual therapy, including massage and passive stretching, is also beneficial. Either ask a friend to massage the area for you or go to a professional masseur. If the muscular tension keeps recurring, it's probably best to seek the advice of a manual practitioner, who can identify the underlying cause.

Exercise can help stretch out and relax tight muscles. It can take the form of prescribed exercise given by your manual practitioner when the problem is more troublesome and acute. Once you have recovered from the original pain or injury, joining a gym, stretch classes or sport can provide more of a long-term solution and prevention.

Muscle tension due to emotional stress is probably best helped by addressing the reasons for the stress. Methods of reducing stress and increasing mental relaxation include modifying stressful personal situations, sharing your concerns with family and friends, balancing work with recreation and holidays, paying attention to good posture, making sure you get sufficient sleep, and practising meditation or yoga or listening to relaxation tapes. The advice of a psychologist experienced in stress reduction techniques may motivate you to change your lifestyle, sometimes more easily than you think.

Osteoarthritis

Osteoarthritis (also known as osteoarthrosis, degenerative arthritis, wear and tear, old age, degeneration and rheumatism) is the most common disease of joints, characterised by wear and thinning of the cartilage layer that covers bone ends and the formation of osteophytes (bony outgrowths) at the margins of the joint. Osteoarthritis occurs in everybody as a natural phenomenon with advancing years. It is the condition which most symbolises aging. (The initials OA conveniently stand for both old age and osteoarthritis.) The condition is really quite benign and no different from developing wrinkles or getting grey hair. It has an unjustified reputation because it is widely, but incorrectly, believed to be painful, and may be confused with other painful and disabling forms of arthritis, such as rheumatoid arthritis.

Incidence

Most people over the age of 50, and perhaps all those over 60, have osteoarthritis to some degree, but few affected joints have symptoms. Joints that develop osteoarthritis are usually those that bear the most weight or are used the most; they include the joints of the hands, knees, hips and spine. In the spine, osteoarthritis affects the small paired facet joints at the back of the vertebrae.

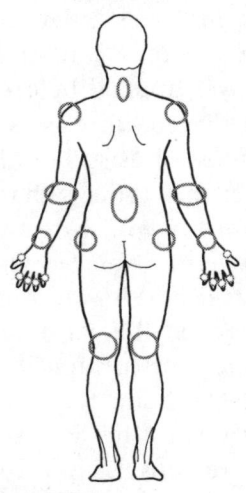

Common sites of osteoarthritis

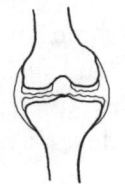

A: Early degeneration with roughing of articular cartilages.

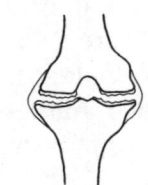

B: Further wear of cartilages with reduced space between bones. Bone more dense under worn cartilages. Bone spurs at joint margins.

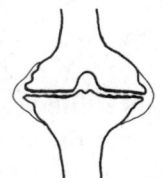

C: Cartilages nearly destroyed, marked joint space narrowing, large bone spurs. Thickened joint capsule.

Stages of osteoarthritis

If osteoarthritis occurs at an early age, it may be due to previous injury (for example a fracture), congenital abnormality (for example, congenital dislocation of the hip), or the development of joint disease like osteochondritis (defective growth of a bone).

Symptoms and signs

The great majority of osteoarthritic joints in older people produce no pain or inflammation and give no trouble at all. In fact, osteoarthritis is not quite the correct term for the condition, since '-itis' indicates inflammation and this form of arthritis is really a 'cold' condition without pain or swelling. The name was applied before the condition was properly understood. Osteoarthrosis is the more accurate name; nevertheless, most of us still call it osteoarthritis.

As joints grow older the cartilage that caps the bone ends gradually becomes worn down. X-rays show the two bones sitting more closely together. The cartilage loses its near frictionless smooth surface, developing a gritty sensation that sounds like sandpaper, as the joint moves, for example, when bending the knees or turning the head. Around the margins of the joint the bone forms arthritic spurs (outgrowths), and underneath the worn cartilage the bone becomes sclerotic (more dense), appearing whiter on X-ray.

As the condition develops, movement becomes increasingly limited. The stiffness is due to the fact that the soft tissues connecting the joint are aging at the same rate. The joint capsule (the bag enveloping the joint) and ligaments become dried out, thickened and less supple. At the same time, the muscles around the joint shrink and lose their elasticity and some strength.

This process, which cannot be seen on X-ray, is vital to understanding why osteoarthritis is regarded as a painful condition when mostly it is not. The aging soft tissues become less supple and weaker, and this makes an osteoarthritic joint more susceptible to injury. Pain and inflammation arises simply because the soft tissues have been mildly sprained.

When pain is present, symptoms resemble those of a joint sprain, except that they develop more easily and resolve more slowly. The stresses of daily living and fatigue can be sufficient to cause symptoms.

Later, as the cartilage becomes more worn down, pain can develop in the underlying bone as it is not as protected by the layer of cartilage. Here, microscopic fractures are thought to be responsible.

Treatment

Osteoarthritic changes cannot be reversed, but since the condition is rarely a threat to continued activity and enjoyment of life, treatment need go only as far as the patient's comfort requires. It is not necessary to accept persistent 'arthritic' pain as a fact of life.

Anti-inflammatory drugs (aspirin-like medication) are the main medical treatment. The newer anti-inflammatory drugs are convenient because they only need to be taken once or twice a day. Glucosamine and chondroitin sulphate, sold as cartilage extract, has been shown to be beneficial. An injection of cortisone mixed with analgesic is occasionally used to help a single joint if it is persistently swollen and painful.

Manual therapy helps a stiff arthritic joint to become more flexible and relaxes tense, complaining muscles. It seems to help the joint tolerate physical stresses better. Treatment is gentle and continued for a little longer than many manual therapy problems. Sometimes maintenance therapy can be helpful.

Other helpful treatments might include heat and cold packs, acupuncture, electrical treatments like ultrasound and interferential electrotherapy, and exercise therapy such as hydrotherapy (water exercises), Feldenkrais (learning easier ways of moving) and Pilates. Naturopathic and homoeopathic medicines may also be of benefit.

It is helpful to spend less time standing and walking when the layer of cartilage is heavily worn and bone pain is contributing to the discomfort. In this case, the pain is slower to resolve. Overweight sufferers will benefit from losing some weight. If the condition is severe, various aids can make coping around the home more manageable.

Most osteoarthritis is quite manageable but advanced cases can lead to persistent, quite severe pain and disability. Although not always successful in completely eliminating pain, surgical treatment has much to offer. Arthroplasty (joint replacement) is available for many joints of the arm and leg.

Rheumatism

Rheumatism is a term used to describe non-specific disorders with pain and stiffness in the muscles and joints. It's generally used by the public rather than professionals. Most practitioners wish the word would disappear, because it is a condition that, strictly speaking, does not exist. In reality, rheumatism is used to describe a hotch-potch of separate diseases where there is pain and stiffness in the muscles and joints. It includes many minor and persistent strains, aches and pains, as well as degenerative disorders such as arthritis and spondylosis.

Most cases of 'rheumatism' are provoked or aggravated by mechanical overload. They are usually excellent cases for manual therapy.

Soft tissue injury

This is a general term to describe damage to the soft tissues, especially muscles, tendons and fascia.

On reflection, you might conclude from what you've read so far that every condition I've described in this book is a type of soft tissue injury. After all, the soft tissues and their treatment are at the core of manual therapy. In that sense you are correct; damage to any one of the five tissues joining the bones could be described as a soft tissue injury.

However, the medical definition of soft tissue injury is

narrower. It is a way of saying that there is no fracture or joint damage. Therefore, injury to ligament, joint capsule (the bag that encloses a joint) or disc, which are parts of a joint but are also soft tissues, are not normally described as soft tissue damage.

Soft tissue injuries to muscles, tendons and fascia are mechanical problems that are well managed by manual practitioners.

Subluxation

The concept of subluxation is a central part of chiropractic. It is the Holy Grail, and at the same time an intensely debated term within the chiropractic profession. Like religion, everybody has his or her own version. Essentially, every mechanical problem in this book might be called a subluxation by a chiropractor.

Classically, a subluxation was viewed by both chiropractic and medicine as a bone out of alignment, although something less than a dislocation. Since then, the definition of chiropractic subluxation has been under continual evolution. The two forms of subluxation are now seen as quite different.

A recent definition of a chiropractic subluxation is 'a motion segment in which alignment, movement integrity and/or physiological function are altered, although contact between the joint surfaces remains intact'.

One problem with this definition is the concept of misalignment. Non-chiropractic terms, such as mechanical disorder, no longer refer to vertebral alignment, as there is no correlation between misalignment and subluxation. Minor variations in vertebral alignment are universal, frequent, non-symptomatic and normal in the population. (See Chapter 5, The great 'bone out of place' controversy.) Moreover, studies demonstrate that manipulation has no effect on the position of a vertebra.

Another difficulty is that it is not possible to define subluxation as a medical entity. Subluxation is not one condition any more than a mechanical disorder, dental problem or psychiatric condition is a single entity. Subluxation is a whole range of conditions with a common means of chiropractic (manual therapy) treatment.

The difficulty of identifying and defining subluxation is not unique. There are about 100 synonyms approximating subluxation. These range from spinal joint blocking, manipulable lesion and somatic dysfunction, to the term 'mechanical disorder', used in this book.

In time it will become increasingly accepted that subluxation and other terms like it are more simply understood by the public as any disorder that responds to manual therapy.

CHAPTER ELEVEN

GENERAL DISORDERS OF THE SPINE

- Intervertebral disc problems ■ Disc sprain
- Disc prolapse ■ Disc degeneration
- Intervertebral joint strain ■ Postural strain
- Pregnancy and the back ■ Scoliosis
- Spondylosis

Intervertebral disc problems

Intervertebral discs are tough fibrous pads between each vertebra, making up about a quarter of the length of the spine. In the lower back, discs consist of a soft gelatinous core, the nucleus pulposis, surrounded by a fibrous ring, the annulus fibrosis.

The disc is very firmly connected to a vertebra above and below. The hard vertebrae alternating with the springy discs make the spine strong but flexible; the discs allow the whole structure to absorb shock and the physical stresses of daily life.

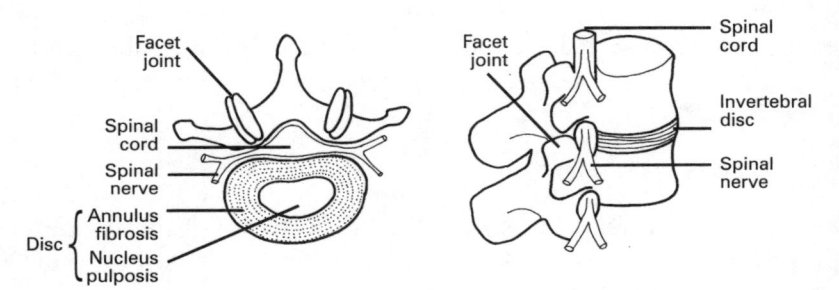

A normal intervertebral disc

Disc lesions have a multitude of names. The disc may be described as sprained, bulging, herniated, protruding, slipped, prolapsed, ruptured, narrowed, thinned, degenerated or disrupted! Don't be alarmed; they are not that complicated. They really fall into three categories. A disc sprain might be called a bulging or slipped disc. A disc prolapse might be described as a disc protrusion or herniation, and a slipped or ruptured disc. A degenerated disc might be narrowed or thinned.

Not all disc problems are painful. The central part of a disc, the nucleus pulposis, has no pain-sensing fibres. Pain is felt only if the layers around the nucleus are damaged. A disc that degenerates and dries out with age is normally painless.

Internal disc disruption is a fourth, more recently accepted disc problem, in which the pulpy centre (nucleus pulposis) of the disc breaks down. It's not really clear why it breaks down or where this leads. It can occur in isolation or develop into one of the other disc troubles.

There are two significant aspects to a disc injury. Firstly, the disc recovers much more slowly than a joint, ligament or muscle injury as it has an extremely poor blood supply. Secondly, a damaged and swollen disc can pinch a nerve, causing sciatic pain in the leg or brachial pain in the arm. Occasionally the pinched nerve needs an operation to relieve it.

The good news is that with increasing age a disc becomes less troublesome. As it dries out, the disc loses its capacity to prolapse. There are enough other things going wrong as we get older, so at least that's one less problem to worry about!

Disc sprain

Disc sprain (also known as disc bulge, sprain of the annulus fibrosis or slipped disc) is the partial tear of the annulus fibrosis (outer ring of the disc) without any leakage of the nucleus pulposis (pulpy centre of the disc). The sprained part of the disc becomes inflamed and swollen, hence 'disc bulge', but the bulge is not sufficient to compress nearby nerves.

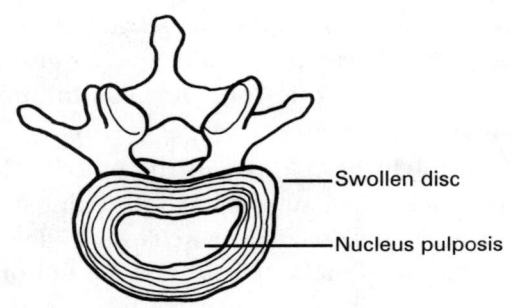

Cross-section of a disc sprain

Causes

Although a disc sprain can be caused by a strenuous action, such as lifting a heavy weight or twisting violently, it is usually the final straw of repeated more minor damage to the back. Consequently, most people suffering from disc sprain have had previous back trouble. Quite often, a disc sprain follows little more than a slight overload when reaching, bending or twisting.

People between the ages of 25 and 40 are more likely to suffer from a disc sprain. Over the age of 25 the discs start to dehydrate, become less resilient and are more prone to strain. After the age of 40, they gain fibrous tissue and become more stable again. A disc sprain is slightly more common in men than in women.

About 90 per cent of disc sprains occur in the lower back. They sometimes develop in the lower neck and are rare in the thoracic spine where the barrel-like rib cage protects the discs from excessive stresses.

Symptoms

A person stooping over a job might feel a minor strain in the back. They stand up and check themselves out but may not feel too bad because the annulus has relatively few pain sensors. They might even finish the job. Then gradually, over the rest of the day or that night, they develop pain and stiffness in the back. Pain increases at a leisurely pace, over 6 to 12 hours, because the annulus fibrosis also has a poor blood supply. It takes this long for painful inflammation and swelling to develop.

Pain might be referred to the buttock, hip or thigh, but there is not sufficient swelling of the disc to pinch the sciatic nerve and cause sciatica. A scoliosis (sideways curvature of the spine) may make the sufferer lean to one side to reduce discomfort. Pain is often worse when sitting and standing, and relieved by lying down.

A disc sprain can have similar symptoms to a sprain of a facet joint, which lies just near the disc. The diagnosis is sometimes made in retrospect, as the poor blood supply to the disc makes healing much slower than a sprained facet joint.

Treatment

In most cases, a disc sprain recovers in one or two weeks. It usually responds to a day or two of rest lying down and anti-inflammatory drugs (aspirin-like medication). Special exercises and some warmth may help reduce muscle spasm and inflammation.

Because a disc sprain is generally the end result of previous repeated damage to that part of the spine, there is often more longstanding muscle fibrosis and joint stiffness. Many manual practitioners believe that if these changes remain untreated, future episodes of disc trouble are more likely to occur. Gentle manual therapy is believed to help restore spinal flexibility and reduce the possibility of future disc trouble.

Disc prolapse

Disc prolapse (also known as disc protrusion, disc herniation, ruptured disc or slipped disc) is a common, painful disorder of the spine, usually a development of repeated disc sprain or perhaps following internal disc disruption (breakdown of the pulpy core). The outer ring of a disc tears and part of its pulpy core protrudes (hence disc protrusion), causing painful and at times disabling pressure on a nerve. It is not possible to literally slip a disc out of position. The term 'slipped disc' was coined before the problem was properly understood.

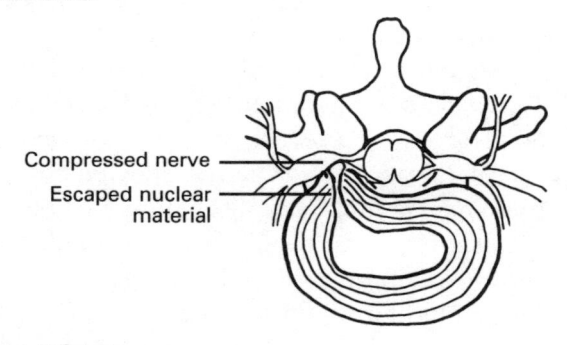

A disc prolapse

Symptoms

A prolapsed disc in the lower back causes sciatica (pain running down the leg due to pressure on the sciatic nerve) and back pain. Tingling, numbness and sometimes weakness in certain muscles of the leg can accompany the sciatica. Sufferers may be unable to straighten up fully or are forced to lean to one side to ease the pain. Coughing, sneezing or laughing often aggravates the pain.

In rare cases, a large lumbar disc prolapse can cause pressure on the spinal cord itself, leading to loss of bladder or bowel control and paralysis of the legs. Urgent surgery is needed for this type of prolapse.

A prolapsed disc in the neck causes brachialgia (pain with tingling and numbness in the arm), neck pain and stiffness, and occasionally weakness in certain muscles of the arm or hand.

Treatment

In most cases, symptoms are relieved by initially resting on a firm mattress for several days up to one or two weeks and by taking anti-inflammatory drugs. Some simple exercises can be done in bed.

Recovery occurs as the protruding material dies and slowly withers away while the torn annulus fibrosis (outer layer of the disc) heals over. Healing is slow because the blood supply to a disc is so limited. It may take several weeks and sometimes months for a severe prolapse to recover.

As the severe pain eases, the patient is allowed out of bed and might attend for manual therapy. Therapy includes such things as heat, traction, ultrasound, massage, mobilisation (small rhythmic oscillations), special exercises and sometimes the prescription of a supportive brace or neck collar.

It is not entirely clear why manual therapy helps a disc prolapse. We know from scans and operations that the protruding tissue does not return back into the disc. It dies and shrivels up over time, shrinking away from the compressed nerve. Manual therapy is less effective if there is not much muscle spasm and joint stiffness. It is therefore suspected that the treatment reduces troublesome pre-existing scar tissue and stiffness that, in some way, weakened the disc and led to its prolapse.

An epidural injection of local anaesthetic (with or without cortisone), given by a medical practitioner, might be recommended to relieve marked sciatic pain, prevent adhesions (scar tissue) from forming and allow earlier manual therapy. The epidural injection is similar to that given during childbirth. In my experience it also greatly relieves the ordeal for the partner!

Occasionally, if the sciatic pain is severe and persistent, if there is muscle weakness and reflex changes, or if bladder or bowel function is impaired, surgery may be needed. The most common operation, a discectomy, removes the offending protrusion. More and more, this procedure is being carried out under a microscope; it is known as a microdiscectomy. The method greatly speeds recovery and reduces complications. The patient can go home the same day or after an overnight stay.

Disc degeneration

Disc degeneration (also known as disc narrowing or disc thinning) is the aging of a disc. Progressive dehydration (reduction in water content) leads to loss of volume and a reduction in the height of a disc when seen on X-ray. Disc degeneration is mostly painless.

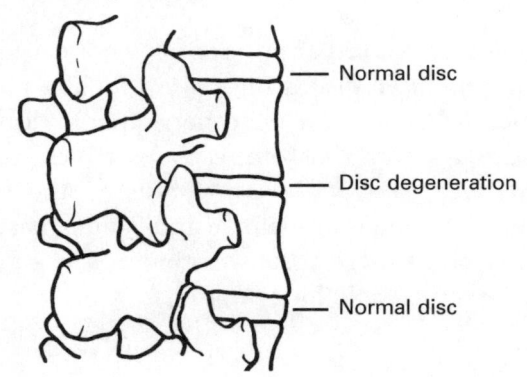

Disc degeneration

Causes

Although the culprit might be previous disc sprain, disc prolapse or disc disruption, the normal cause is simple aging. In fact, 75 per cent of the population over the age of 50 has some disc degeneration in their spines. Here, the disc is less able to attract and hold fluid. As it dries out, the body weight squashes it and the disc becomes noticeably thinner or 'narrowed' when viewed on X-ray. Disc degeneration is one of several reasons why we shrink as we grow older. Other reasons include loss of height of the vertebra and the tendency to become more stooped over. Disc degeneration often accompanies spondylosis (aging of the spine), and symptoms, when present, are indistinguishable.

The presence of disc degeneration under the age of 40 suggests that there has been a previous injury to the disc. Sometimes disc narrowing is congenital (present from birth). In this case the narrowing can be seen on X-ray, and is confined to a single disc.

Symptoms

It may come as a surprise to many, but disc degeneration happens mostly without pain and is an aging process no different to the hair going grey or wrinkles appearing on the face.

When symptoms are present, it's not easy to be sure that the degenerated disc is the reason for the pain. Often, it is blamed when there's no other apparent cause. However, muscle, ligament and joint capsule, which can't be seen on X-ray, wear out at the same rate, so the whole 'motion segment' becomes less supple and is more easily overloaded. Any or all of these tissues, including the degenerated disc, may be responsible for symptoms.

Treatment

Disc degeneration has no cure and cannot be reversed. However, since degeneration occurs mostly without symptoms, treatment need only restore painless mobility.

Gentle, well-focused manual therapy is highly beneficial. It softens, lengthens and loosens all the tissues connecting the two vertebrae, including the disc, and allows the 'segment' to recover painless mobility and cope with future physical activity with much less complaint.

Other treatment may include application of heat, and exercises. Hydrotherapy (water exercises) can gently build flexibility and strength. A light elastic corset or brace may be worn temporarily to reduce strain during gardening or other strenuous activity.

Medical treatment includes the prescription of anti-inflammatory drugs. Overweight people will usually benefit from losing weight so they have less to carry around.

Some people with severe disc degeneration are never free of symptoms despite trying everything. It may be necessary to consider combining the best of the treatments you have already had. Maintenance manual therapy visits can be of great benefit, as well as exercise, losing weight and taking medication, including some naturopathic products.

Intervertebral joint strain

Intervertebral joint strain (also known as facet joint strain, somatic dysfunction, subluxation, misalignment or bone out of place) is a common spinal problem characterised by pain, muscle spasm and stiffness of a single intervertebral joint. Intervertebral strain has long been the cornerstone and staple diet of manual practitioners.

An intervertebral strain goes by an amazing array of names. It may be called facet joint strain, segmental strain, chiropractic subluxation, osteopathic lesion, bone out of place, misalignment, minor mechanical derangement, lumbago, fixation, locking, somatic dysfunction, manipulable lesion or ricked joint. The public and at times the manual professions can be quite bewildered by the variety. The alphabet soup of terms in part reflects the fact that the detail of many back problems is still poorly understood.

Causes and symptoms

Most intervertebral strains begin with a sudden pain in the back or neck. The trigger can be as minor as cleaning one's teeth, sneezing, coughing, reaching out or standing up, or the strain may be caused by a more strenuous activity such as lifting, gardening or pushing furniture about. Sometimes there is no apparent cause — the muscles just clench up.

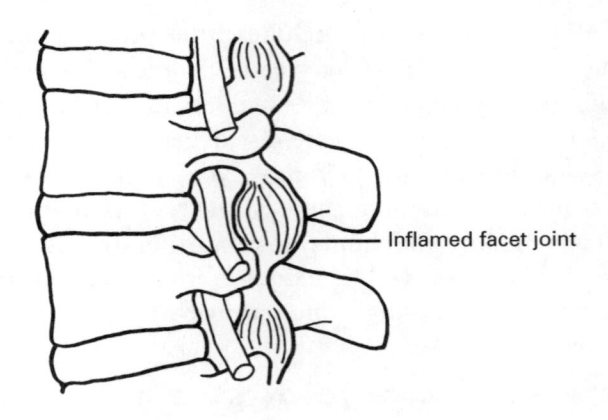

— Inflamed facet joint

Intervertebral joint with inflamed capsule

The result is localised pain and a sense of locking. The small muscles connecting two vertebrae become tight with spasm, the joint becomes stiff and there is tenderness concentrated at one fingertip spot. Press it and the pain is reproduced. You have put your back out! No wonder 'something out of place' is a favourite expression; it's exactly what it feels like.

It is not possible to be sure exactly which structure (joint capsule, ligament or muscle) is damaged; more than one may be injured at the same time. Nor is the reason for the persistence of this tightly focused spasm and stiffness clear. The manual professions have investigated it for years. Two major theories have emerged; one or both of them might be valid.

The first theory concentrates on joint menisci. These are small, delicate frills that extend a short distance into the gap between the joint surfaces. It is thought that a meniscus can become nipped, causing pain, muscle spasm and locking in a similar way to a torn meniscus (cartilage) in the knee. Manipulation is thought to release the little meniscus, allowing it to move back to its proper place, and resolve the pain, spasm and locking.

The second, older theory, although still popular, suggests that muscle spasm jams the complicated movement patterns between two vertebrae like a stuck drawer. In this hypothesis, manipulation shifts the axis of movement and unblocks the obstruction. The painful spasm subsides as soon as movement is restored, giving the immediate feeling of, 'Ah, that's back in place!'

Treatment

The pain and stiffness of an intervertebral strain rarely lasts for more than a few days. However, repeated episodes can lead to residual stiffness, which increases the chance of further bouts and a slower recovery on each occasion. Ultimately, this can result in persistent mild discomfort interspersed with acute episodes. Osteopaths and chiropractors believe the reduced mobility impairs fluid exchange to the disc causing increased likelihood of disc trouble.

Manual therapy is the most effective method of treating intervertebral strain. The instantaneous relief following manipulation has nothing to do with a bone being realigned — this does not happen. It is more to do with the capacity for manipulation to focus therapy on the 'unisegmental' soft tissues at fault. The restoration of movement and reduction of painful muscle spasm is the most likely reason for relief.

Other treatment might include anti-inflammatory drugs, temporary rest, application of heat, ultrasound, exercises and sometimes acupuncture. In some cases, an injection of local anaesthetic mixed with cortisone may be recommended.

Postural strain

A good posture consists of efficiently balancing the body weight down through the bones of the body. It depends on the shape of the spine and the balanced support of ligament and muscle 'guy lines'. Maintaining a good posture helps prevent neck and back pain.

A stooped or slouched posture reduces the vertical arrangement of the bones and puts greater stress on the supporting ligaments and muscles. This might result in what is termed 'postural strain'.

Despite the moral disdain often evoked by 'bad posture', whether inherited or acquired, it can be perfectly comfortable. Appearances can deceive and a posture that causes pain in one person will not necessarily produce discomfort in another.

Good posture is really a position that is comfortable for that person (no aches, pains or other symptoms), and that

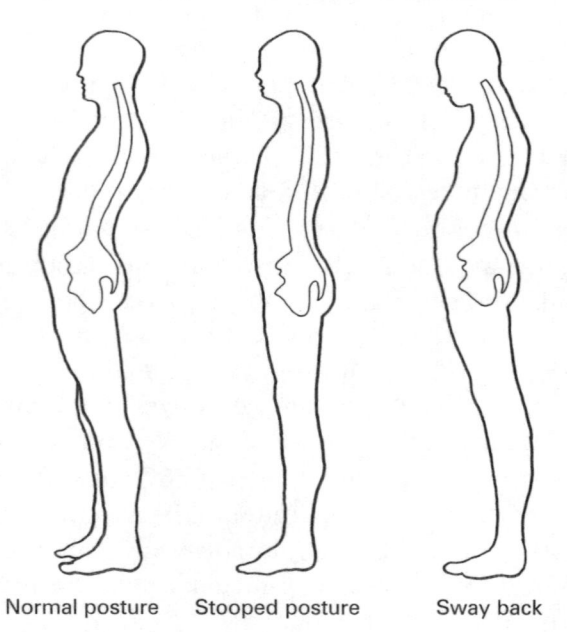

Normal posture   Stooped posture   Sway back

Different types of posture

has no negative effects. In other words, the posture should neither fatigue the muscles nor strain the joints.

Manual practitioners often treat people with 'bad posture'. Once treated, the pain disappears but the posture remains. This is true of most painful back problems diagnosed as postural strains.

Interestingly, these people, once cured of their back pain, usually say that their posture has improved and that they are sitting and standing more erect. But this is really an illusion caused by the reduction of pain and improved flexibility. Accurate measurement of the spine demonstrates little change takes place in postural curves.

This is not to say that manual treatment, exercises and other advice for postural strain are wasted goals. They are entirely worthwhile and will greatly help reduce backache and prevent further deterioration. However, in the end, manual therapy, exercises or other treatment, directed at changing posture while relieving pain and stiffness, and helping to minimise deterioration, does little to physically alter the shape of the back.

Sway back

Sway back (hollow back) is a posture where a person stands with the pelvis forward and the abdomen protruding. As the trunk leans back, the shoulders slump forward to counterbalance it. Also known as hollow back, this is a common example of what is considered to be bad posture.

Parents are often concerned that sway back in their children either leads to or is the cause of backache. It can disturb some parents for aesthetic or social reasons. They believe children should stand up straight, look people in the eye and show some self-respect.

A sway back posture is mostly inherited and is similar to that of a near relative at the same age. Other causes include obesity, compensation for pregnancy and possibly an expression of defiance or chronic discontent.

Most books on the subject describe various methods of improving the posture, which will in turn relieve backache. By doing yoga, exercises or Alexander technique, or by developing postural awareness people may hold a new posture for a few minutes and gradually extend this to become the normal pattern.

These methods do help if there is pain or stiffness but do little to change posture. It may be wiser, easier and quicker to use manual therapy to loosen and relieve the complaining joints, and ignore the postural issues. In fact, most teenagers will grow out of their 'bad posture' as their bodies develop adult proportions.

The issue of sway back can be dealt with by approaching it sideways. If it is an unconscious expression of poor self-esteem, it may be overcome by developing a new interest. Joining a gym or taking up jazz ballet, karate, water polo or any activity requiring participation can fire enthusiasm and help develop more flexible ways of moving.

Pregnancy and the back

Manual therapy has much to offer pre- and post-natal women. Back pain during pregnancy is common, as the process of pregnancy puts tremendous demands on the lower back, the mid thoracic (between the shoulder blades) and cervical spine (neck).

Lower back pain is the most common complaint, particularly during the last three months of pregnancy, when fatigue, mechanical loading, altered posture and ligamentous laxity are at their most pronounced. For some, sciatica can be a problem. As a woman's posture changes, she may find she becomes more round-shouldered and experiences discomfort in her upper back or neck.

Mechanical strains on the body framework during pregnancy might contribute to headaches, respiratory distress, circulatory problems, fatigue, nausea and indigestion. Gentle manual therapy might be applicable in all of these problems.

Labour itself is an extremely strenuous process and can result in persistent lower back pain, particularly when there has been a previous history of back trouble. Coccydinia (coccyx pain) may follow due to strain on coccygeal attachments or the lower back joints.

Coping with a new baby can be exceedingly fatiguing. The interruption of sleep and unaccustomed bending and lifting is added to the exhaustion of the earlier pregnancy and labour. It is not surprising that backache can occur at this time.

Medication and X-ray investigation are not generally acceptable for back trouble during pregnancy. However, manual therapy can gently help the musculoskeletal framework to accommodate to the increasing demands of the growing foetus. After delivery, manual treatment is highly beneficial; it can assist the body to return to normality and prevent the development of long-term back pain.

Scoliosis

Scoliosis is a sideways curvature of the spine that can be seen when viewed from the back. In many cases, a nearby area of the spine compensates by curving back in the opposite direction, so the spine appears to be S-shaped. The thoracic (chest) and lumbar (lower back) spine are the most commonly affected.

Types

An 'antalgic (pain-relieving) scoliosis' is a temporary scoliosis where a person bends more to one side in order to ease pain caused by a back problem, such as a sprained disc. In this case, the spinal curvature disappears as soon as the injury recovers.

A 'short leg' can tilt the pelvis and result in a scoliosis. This is due to the legs finishing their growth at slightly different lengths. Occasionally a fracture can result in one leg remaining shorter than the other. Rarely, osteomyelitis (a bone infection) in one leg stunts its growth.

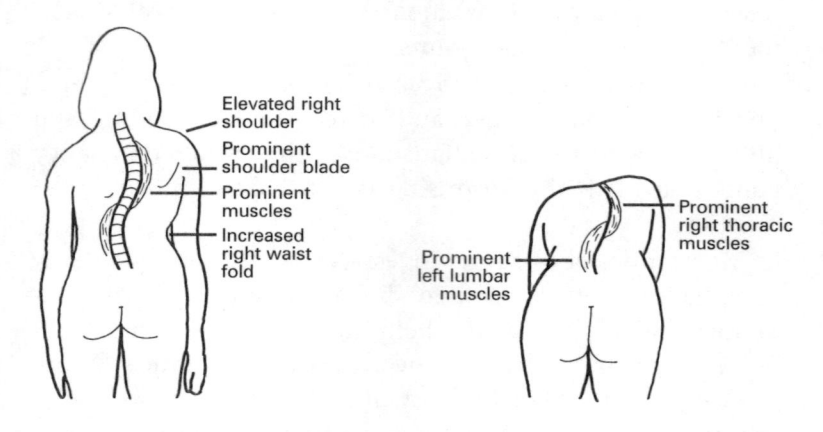

Idiopathic scoliosis, standing and bending

'Idiopathic scoliosis' is more common in girls. It develops in childhood or early adolescence and its cause is unknown. The S-shaped curvature becomes more marked until the age at which growth stops. It occasionally becomes a severe problem, with the deformity requiring surgical correction. It is recommended that checks be made for the condition in all children at the ages of 11 and 13. Rarely it becomes sufficiently severe to require surgical correction. Polio, now very rare, can weaken the back muscles on one side and lead to a similar scoliosis.

Symptoms and signs

Scoliosis is diagnosed by physical examination of the spine, hips and legs, along with an X-ray examination of the spine.

Back pain, muscle spasm and, sometimes, sciatica (pain down the leg) accompany antalgic (pain-relieving) scoliosis. A disc sprain is the most common cause. The other two types of scoliosis (short leg and idiopathic) usually have no symptoms at all and might be spotted by an observant parent watching their child play.

Idiopathic scoliosis can be recognised when looking at the back in a bent-over position. A high side or hump can be seen on one side of the thoracic (chest) or lumbar (lower back) spine.

People complaining of back pain can incorrectly be told that their pain is due to a curvature. However, studies show that people with mild to moderate idiopathic scoliosis experience no more backache than people with normal backs. So idiopathic scoliosis is not usually a cause of backache. When back pain does develop it is for reasons other than the scoliosis, and the curvature is only coincidentally present.

Treatment

Antalgic scoliosis requires treatment directed to the cause — usually a disc sprain. Treatment might include temporary bed rest, analgesic medication (pain-killers) and measures such as manual therapy and physiotherapy.

A short leg scoliosis rarely needs treatment, although a built-up shoe might be recommended if the imbalance is severe.

Idiopathic (unknown origin) scoliosis will not need treatment in most cases when the curvature is mild to moderate. However, six monthly measurement of the curve, during the growth phase, might be necessary to check whether the curve is progressing. Manual therapy cannot help this type of scoliosis. Rarely, surgery is required to straighten severe idiopathic scoliosis. This is done to avoid a gradual deterioration, breathing difficulties and heart problems in old age.

In summary, back pain may be the reason for a curvature (antalgic scoliosis) or it may have nothing to do with it (short leg and idiopathic scoliosis). In both cases, manual therapy helps the pain. In the former, the pain and curvature resolve together; in the latter, the pain subsides but not the curvature.

Spondylosis

Spondylosis is aging of the spine, usually without symptoms. It is also known as arthritis of the spine, spinal degeneration, wear and tear, rheumatism, old age and spondylosis deformans. It is diagnosed by X-ray and characterised by bony spurs (outgrowths) called osteophytes that develop on the rim of a vertebral body. Spondylosis quite often accompanies disc degeneration.

Incidence

Equal numbers of men and women are affected by spondylosis. It starts to develop between the ages of 40 and 50, about a decade earlier than osteoarthritis. Factors that might lead to spondylosis at an earlier age include recurrent intervertebral joint strain, disc prolapse, fracture and Scheuermann's disease (defective growth of the vertebral bodies).

The levels of the spine most commonly affected are those in the lower lumbar spine, the mid to lower neck, and the mid thoracic spine.

Symptoms

As is the case with other disorders of wear and tear, such as osteoarthritis, spondylosis is usually evidence of advancing years. Most people who have the condition do not suffer from pain or inflammation.

When symptoms develop, they arise not from the spondylitic bones seen on X-ray but from the nearby muscles, ligaments and fascia. These soft tissues age at the same rate as bone. They dry out and lose their elasticity and movements become less supple. They become susceptible to the strains of bending, twisting and physical activity. An X-ray showing spondylosis is really an indication of aging in the soft tissues. To a manual practitioner, spondylosis seen on an X-ray really shows the tendency of the soft tissues to give trouble.

The only symptom a person may suffer is occasional stiffness, which is ignored. Pain might develop at times of increased physical effort, such as when gardening or vacuuming, and then subside between. Occasionally a bony spur can narrow the exit hole of a spinal nerve and cause pressure with tingling and numbness in the region it supplies.

Treatment

The bony appearance of spondylosis has no cure and cannot be reversed. However, symptoms, when present, respond well to a manual therapy approach, as they arise from the soft tissues that connect the bones.

There are numerous anti-inflammatory drugs that are used to treat spondylosis. In a severe attack, temporary rest by lying down will help to settle the pain. Overweight people should try to reduce their weight.

Manual treatment reduces pain and stiffness by restoring flexibility to the soft tissues and joints. Manual practitioners believe that this treatment also slows down the progression of spondylosis. In minor cases, mobility is easily improved. More troublesome cases might require treatment over a longer period. Sometimes symptoms never completely recover. In this case, maintenance manual therapy might be necessary. Heat treatment, special home exercises, hydrotherapy (water exercises) or stretch classes might also be helpful.

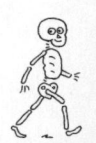

HEAD SYMPTOMS

CHAPTER TWELVE

- Ear symptoms ■ Eye symptoms ■ Migraine
- Post-traumatic headache ■ Psychological symptoms ■ Sinus pain ■ Snoring
- Temporomandibular (jaw) joint disfunction
- Tension headaches ■ Vertigo

Headache is one of the most frequent painful complaints for which a doctor is consulted. It can cause fear and alarm in those who suffer from regular or severe headaches. They might be afraid that they have an undiagnosed brain tumour or some other serious disorder. Fortunately, a headache is only very occasionally a symptom of a serious underlying condition. A busy medical practitioner might see a brain tumour every five or ten years.

In a given year, 80 per cent of women and 65 per cent of men will experience at least one headache. About 35 per cent of women and 20 per cent of men suffer from recurrent headaches. But only 1–2 per cent of the population will consult their family doctor about their headache in that year. Many people live with their problem, accepting their headaches, self-medicating and thinking that little more can be done.

Most people who complain of headache can be assessed and successfully treated by manual practitioners. The upper neck causes or makes a significant contribution to the great proportion of headaches. All of the conditions in this chapter are related to mechanical factors in the neck that provoke or aggravate headaches. In each case, manual therapy is beneficial and often the treatment of choice.

The upper neck causes a wider range of head symptoms than most people realise. Every part of the head, except the nose, chin, lips and pinna (ear flaps), can experience pain referred from the neck.

If you suffer from headaches, you might have already noticed pain, tension, stiffness and tenderness in the upper neck under the back of the skull. To check for yourself, try pushing your thumb underneath the skull, shrug your shoulders tightly or roll your head round. Does your upper neck feel tender, tight or stiff? Does this bring on or affect the symptoms? If so, your neck could be the reason for your headache.

A manual practitioner takes particular care when treating the upper neck. The two top spinal joints are relatively inaccessible, as they are tucked away between the jaw in front and the base of the skull behind. A high level of manual skill is needed to localise effective treatment to this region.

Ear symptoms

Earache

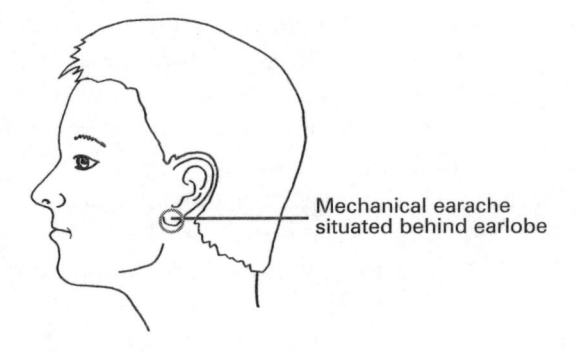

Mechanical earache situated behind earlobe

The location of mechanical earache

Pain in the ear can be one of the most distressing symptoms. Most earaches originate in the ear itself and require medical treatment. However, sometimes pain that seems to be coming from the ear can arise from a mechanical problem in the upper neck.

If this is the case, the discomfort is not located deep inside the ear like an infection, but immediately behind the ear lobe, in the gap between the jaw and the skull. The pain is caused by spasm of the muscles attaching to the side of the top neck vertebra. Prod gently and you might locate the pain. It feels like a tender enlarged gland. If you are not sure, consult your medical practitioner. Assessment and treatment by a manual practitioner may be better if you also have neck pain, muscular tension and headaches, or a previous history of these symptoms.

Tinnitus

Tinnitus is the perception of sound in the absence of an exterior stimulus. You might hear buzzing, ringing, roaring, whistling or hissing. It can be low- or high-pitched, continuous or intermittent.

There are many known causes for tinnitus, of which aging is the most common. Other reasons include excessive wax, high blood pressure, otosclerosis (an ear defect that leads to hearing loss), Meniere's syndrome (an inner ear affliction that disturbs hearing and balance), head trauma, and drugs such as aspirin, quinine and streptomycin. In many cases, the cause cannot be identified and this makes treatment very difficult.

Mechanical disorders are an unusual cause of tinnitus; people rarely think of manual therapy as a possible treatment. But occasionally, treatment for an upper neck problem will reduce or remove the noise.

A trial of manual therapy should be considered if you find head position or movement affects the tinnitus, or if there is muscle tension, tenderness and decreased mobility of the upper neck.

With so many causes, manual therapists can't be sure that they will improve the tinnitus. Indeed, the connection is not well understood. If a mechanical disorder in the upper neck is a factor in a particular case, the tinnitus should start improving, like most mechanical problems, within a three-treatment trial.

Eye symptoms

Osteopaths and chiropractors believe that mechanical disorders in the upper neck cause three types of eye problem: blurred vision, eye pain and twitching of an eyelid. You might wish to check first with your optometrist or eye specialist to see whether there is an eye problem. If there is not, a manual practitioner may be able to help.

Blurred vision

Blurred vision, or loss of acuity (sharpness of vision), is the most frequent eye disturbance seen by both ophthalmic (eye) practitioners and manual practitioners; however, they treat quite different problems. Refraction and focusing disorders of the eye are diagnosed and treated by an optometrist. They will identify if the blurring is due to the eyes and if glasses or other treatment are indicated. If you don't need new glasses and the optometrist cannot explain your blurred vision, you may be left wondering what to do. Most optometrists and medical practitioners are quite unaware that the upper neck is a common cause of blurred vision.

A sufferer can usually work out if blurring is due to a problem in their neck. Their eyes drift slightly out of focus intermittently, particularly when working on the computer, watching TV or looking down to read, write or sew. Blinking brings the world back into focus, but it slides readily back into a blur. There is tension, stiffness, pain and tenderness under the base of the skull and sometimes headaches. Pushing your thumb up under the base of the skull and doing neck exercises relieves the blurring. An optometrist will say that the eyes do not account for the problem, while a manual practitioner will confirm muscular tension and stiffness in the upper neck.

Pain

Mechanical disorders in the upper neck can give referred pain to one or both eyes. The pain is a deep, boring ache within or behind the eyes. Sometimes there is an alarming sharp stab of pain in one eye, which can come from nowhere.

Mechanical eye pain is another variation of tension headache and, like all tension headaches, it tends to come and go for exactly the same reasons. Moreover, the eye pain is accompanied by upper neck discomfort similar to that for blurring and the absence of any eye problem upon visiting the optometrist.

Twitching (flickering) eyelid

This annoying buzzing, vibration or twitching in the upper or lower eyelid tends to occur more with age. Sometimes it feels like tightness around the eye or makes it partially close. Sometimes the twitch is in a facial muscle, particularly the cheek. It is quite distracting and people can feel self-conscious about it as they think the small movement is visible to onlookers.

The problem happens when a group of muscle fibres within the orbicular (eyelid) muscle contract. Although it was traditionally thought to be due to fatigue, it is generally caused by a mechanical disorder in the upper neck.

Treatment

When blurred vision, eye pain or a twitching eyelid has a mechanical origin, manual therapy is directed mainly to the upper two or three neck joints and surrounding muscles. Like most muscular contractions, if there is a twitching eye or face muscle, this also needs gentle massage.

Other treatments might include self-massage or a professional massage to the muscles of the neck, particularly under the base of the skull where the thumbs can be pushed up into this region; special exercises for the upper neck; adequate rest; and paracetamol-type medication.

Migraine

A migraine is a severe kind of throbbing headache that affects 12 per cent of Australians. It generally lasts from 4 to 48 hours and tends to be inherited. About 75 per cent of sufferers are women. The pain is unilateral, only affecting one side, but it can change sides from time to time. There are usually warning symptoms of an oncoming headache such as blurred vision, flickering, bright spots and zigzag lines before the eyes. During an attack, sufferers may have photophobia (an inability to stand bright lights), most feel nauseated and some actually vomit. Sometimes there is tingling or numbness in the region of the mouth, face and hands. Most sufferers having recurrent attacks at varying intervals over many years.

Manual therapy

Chiropractors and osteopaths have claimed for a century that manual therapy helps migraine. Until 1978 the conventional view was that if you did respond to manual treatment then you were not suffering from migraine alone but from a combination of migraine and tension headaches, and that manual therapy only helped the tension headache component. In the 1970s a study took place which threw this view into doubt. It suggested that manual therapy also has a beneficial effect on genuine migraine episodes. Whichever view is correct is not so important in the end. Most sufferers of migraine benefit from manual therapy.

If manual therapy does indeed help the migraine itself, we are not sure exactly why. Some think that mechanical faults are just one of many factors that trigger an attack in a person with an inherited predisposition to migraine. In each attack the upper neck muscles become tense and repeated attacks cause a build-up of tightness, which does not fully subside between episodes. This abnormal state is thought to initiate subsequent migraine attacks. Loosening the muscles and freeing the joints seems to improve the situation.

A manual practitioner will be able to give some indication at your very first visit on the amount of help that you might receive. If he or she finds significant upper neck tension and stiffness you are likely to find that manual therapy will help. Where the physical problem is minor, you probably won't receive so much relief, but the results are not always predictable, so it is sensible to have a short trial of treatment. Three sessions should be enough.

For most people, the frequency, duration, disability and amount of medication used will reduce following manual therapy. A few people will be cured completely, even though the fundamental cause is not physical. In these cases, the patient's body might have reduced its sensitivity to other factors such as diet, stress or hormonal balance, so they no longer trigger an attack; but the mechanical problem is still enough to start a migraine.

Many migraine patients are also aware that they suffer from tension headaches. These people are most likely to obtain improvement from manual therapy because the tension headaches themselves indicate a neck problem.

Even though a manual practitioner will be gentle, the manipulation itself can trigger an attack and sometimes deter a patient from further treatment. If this were to occur, it is usually on the first visit. Fortunately it shows that mechanical factors are important, and means that the treatment is more likely to be successful.

Post-traumatic headache

This is a diffusely distributed headache, very similar to a tension headache, and follows a blow to the head. Post-traumatic headaches might be accompanied by inability to concentrate, lightheadedness or giddiness and intermittent blurred vision.

The word 'concussion' is to be avoided and is incorrect. True concussion is the brief loss of consciousness that usually lasts for only a few seconds following a violent blow to the head. The blow causes minor reversible damage to the brain tissue and temporary interruption to brain function. Symptoms that develop immediately after the incident include confusion and dizziness, with a variable loss of memory about the events immediately preceding the injury. There is always a headache, which disappears after a few hours or days and does not last more than a month. True concussion is definitely NOT an indication for manual therapy.

Of those who have suffered concussion and require hospitalisation, between one-third and one-half develop headaches that continue for more than one month. These 'post-traumatic headaches' are not due to concussion and are rarely due to residual brain injury. Most are headaches referred from the upper neck and a form of muscle contraction headache. In this case, the blow to the head has also injured the junction between the head and neck, causing muscular tension and stiffness, and subsequent referred headaches.

A post-traumatic headache can also follow a more minor blow to the head, such as occurs in sporting collisions, a motor accident or perhaps standing up under a solid object. They might recur for several months or longer. They are brought on by certain head postures, such as prolonged looking downwards or upwards, and aggravated by pressure on tender areas under the base of the skull.

Manual therapy is particularly effective at reaching and freeing up the inaccessible regions under the skull; sometimes it is the only treatment that can bring relief.

Psychological symptoms

Mild depression is the most common emotional response to chronic pain. Since pain is the most frequent symptom treated by manual practitioners, it's not surprising that many of the conditions we see have psychological consequences. Other instances of improved mental performance following manual therapy to the neck include improved concentration span and memory and a general sense of well-being.

Mild depression

Depression gives a sense of 'flatness' accompanied by a loss of drive, vitality and enjoyment of social activities. Prominent symptoms include bodily aches and pains, excessive fatigue, restless sleep and an inability to concentrate.

There are biological, social and psychological causes of depression. Most people experience depression occasionally, often as a normal response to a particular event, such as the death of a near relative. Chronic painful mechanical disorders frequently provoke mild depression but they play no part in more severe depressive illness.

Headaches and neck pain seem to have a particular capacity to cause feelings of mild depression and despondency. Dr Jim Lance, an Australian neurologist, claims that 80 per cent of patients who have tension headaches also suffer from mild depression. A patient with a mechanical disorder in the neck might experience a sense of reduced emotional well-being, feel flat, find they can't concentrate, feel 'woolly' in the head or have a sense of light-headedness and floating.

Quite frequently, a patient having neck treatment will explain that they felt mentally flat or mildly depressed before they sought advice. They are surprised by how much better they feel following manual treatment.

In cases where it is difficult to distinguish between physical or psychological causes of pain accompanying depression, the answer becomes apparent during treatment. When a mechanical problem is the reason, the pain and psychological well-being improves rapidly with manual therapy. If the mental state is producing the physical pain, the depression will not lift as we treat the musculoskeletal system and neither will the pain.

Anger

Negativity, hostility, anger and tantrums are common and almost normal accompaniments to persistent pain, so successful treatment can greatly improve a person's demeanour. The emotional high and sense of well-being following manual treatment can be quite dramatic. Patients frequently recognise their improvement when their family says that they have become much more pleasant to live with.

Poor concentration

Inability to concentrate on a task for any length of time is commonly reported in association with tension headache and neck stiffness. Patients may also describe sensations of feeling woolly-headed, light-headed or floating. These sensations of the mind, while not marked, are disturbing and a constant annoying reminder that all is not well.

Sometimes psychological symptoms are present without the person realising that they have an upper neck problem. At other times, people might comment on their improvement following manual therapy. Once the relationship is established, patients can recognise that upon reappearance of their psychological symptoms their neck needs treatment.

Sinus pain

Sinusitis

Sinusitis is an inflammation of the membrane lining the air cavities around the nose. Most sinusitis is caused by an infection spreading from the nose and is a sequel to the common cold. On rare occasions it can be caused by a tooth infection breaking through into the maxillary (cheek) sinus. Many people think hay fever is a form of sinusitis. This allergic response to pollens and other irritants is really a reaction of the lining to the nose; its medical name is allergic rhinitis.

Dr De Wees, an ear, nose and throat (ENT) specialist and authority on sinusitis, says that out of every 100 people who consult an ENT specialist because of 'sinus trouble', fewer than 10 have sinusitis. So that means more than 90 per cent of patients with sinus trouble are *not* suffering from sinusitis!

Sinusitis is, in fact, vastly over-diagnosed. It has become a

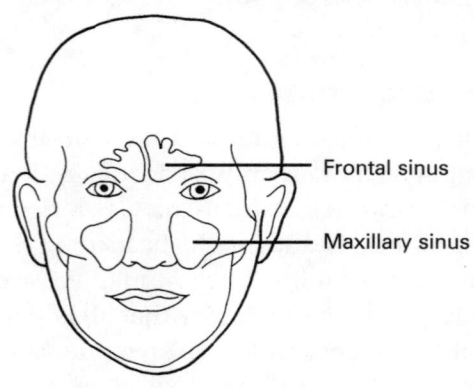

The location of the sinuses

kind of disease demon and a convenient label for blocked noses, hay fever, headaches, sinus pains and sore throats. Misconceived advertising, self-diagnosis, misdiagnosis and claims that manual therapy can help sinusitis have contributed to much of the misunderstanding about the condition.

Mechanical sinus pain

It is most important to distinguish between the 10 per cent true and 90 per cent false sinus troubles, because manual therapy is not of much help for the real thing. However, it is highly beneficial for many of the 90 per cent who suffer sinus pain and who think they have sinusitis.

The best way to test for sinusitis is the hanky test. If you have a streaming nose with clear watery secretion and a soaking wet hankie at times of high pollen count, you probably have hay fever. If you are producing a thick yellow or green, sometimes blood-tinged discharge when you blow your nose it is likely to be infectious sinusitis.

Mechanical 'sinusitis' has no discharge into a hankie, however hard you blow. The chief complaint is of pain. This is felt in the frontal sinuses above the eyes or maxillary sinuses in the cheeks. This sinus pain is really another kind of muscle contraction headache arising from mechanical faults in the upper neck. Manual practitioners have contributed to the confusion about sinusitis. Some practitioners claim to help sinusitis when in fact they only help some of the 90 per cent who think they have it.

True sinusitis sufferers tend to regard any headache over the face or forehead as sinusitis, irrespective of its real cause. Moreover, genuine sufferers gradually seem to develop muscular tension and stiffness in the neck. Like migraine, chronic sinusitis can lead to neck muscle tension, which then refers pain to the sinuses. It might be necessary to consult a manual practitioner to sort out whether there is additional mechanical sinus pain.

Snoring

While the snorer sleeps soundly, the listener hears the symptoms of a condition that afflicts only the unafflicted — the complaint about which only the non-complainers complain! The sleep disturbance to partners, family and even friends can be extremely annoying. Ten per cent of adults snore loudly enough to be heard in the next room.

In snoring, the soft tissues at the back of the mouth become a partial obstruction and vibrate. Many snorers are overweight, with enlarged and limp tissues around the tonsils and uvula.

When a snorer lies on their back, some snoring can be reduced or stopped by simply increasing the height of the pillow. This finding has led to the development of antisnoring pillows that alter the head position, widening the airway sufficiently to prevent snoring.

Regular loud snoring will not respond to manual therapy. The airways are already too narrowed and medical advice is needed. However, if you snore intermittently, more so when you are tired, overdoing it and fatigued, or when you have upper neck tension, stiffness or headaches, or when you consume alcohol or after a long hard drive, then muscular tension may be the cause. The tension alters the head posture and narrows the airway sufficiently to be a partial obstruction. Assessment and treatment by a manual practitioner can help reduce this annoying problem for your partner.

Temporomandibular (jaw) joint disfunction

This condition is characterised by jaw joint pain; sometimes there is pain, clicking and limited ability to open the mouth. The problem can arise from the jaw joint, the muscles that control the jaw joint or the upper neck.

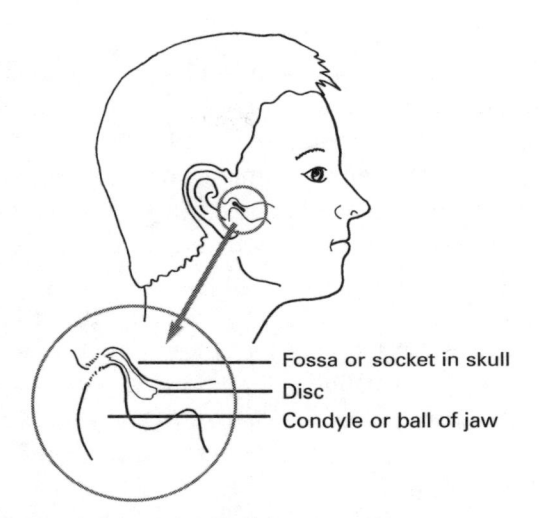

- Fossa or socket in skull
- Disc
- Condyle or ball of jaw

The location of the temporomandibular (jaw) joint

Causes

Joint, jaw and head pain can develop due to prolonged and excessive tension of the chewing muscles. There are believed to be three main reasons for this, which require careful diagnosis. They include abnormalities of bite due to tooth and jaw alignment, tooth grinding at night (bruxism), and mechanical disorders in the upper neck. Psychological stress may be a secondary contributory factor. In some cases, an injury, such as a blow to the jaw, yawning or biting too widely, can strain the joint or cause the disc inside the joint to click.

Diagnosis and treatment of jaw problems can be difficult because the jaw overlaps two professional areas, dentistry and manual therapy. Dentists are trained in bite and tooth-grinding problems but are not usually trained to assess and treat the neck. A dentist might choose only between bite and grinding problems as the cause of jaw pain, without being completely satisfied that the neck is not causing the trouble.

Treatment

If the reason for your jaw pain is unclear to your dentist, you could suggest a cooperative approach between the dentist and a manual practitioner. You could ask your dentist if he or she is sure the dental problem accounts for the pain or whether it would be worth consulting a manual practitioner before embarking on a splint or more major dentistry. The manual practitioner can quickly and easily check for and treat a neck problem causing jaw pain. It could save you pain, time, cost and even a bit of embarrassment.

A strained joint usually settles down within a few hours or days. If slow to recover, it can be treated with manual therapy and exercises, which gently stretch and free up the uncomfortable movements.

Tension headaches

Tension headaches (also known as muscle contraction headache or cervical headache) cause pain affecting the back, top, side or front of the head, due to excessive tension of the muscles attaching under the base of the skull.

There is a medical adage that says: 'Common things occur commonly', and this is particularly true of tension headache, the most common of all headaches. As many as 90 per cent of all headaches are tension headaches.

Causes

Anything that knots up the back of the neck has the potential to cause a tension headache. Physical strain and mental fatigue are the two major reasons for tension headaches.

Common physical reasons include holding the neck in a sustained, unaccustomed or awkward position, such as when using a computer, doing prolonged deskwork, taking a long car trip, sewing, painting the ceiling or skirting boards, or talking to somebody or watching the television with the head turned for too long.

Mental fatigue can result from work pressure, too many late nights, getting run down and burnt out, having personal and emotional worry, being over-commited and generally having too much on your plate.

It can be difficult to distinguish between a tension headache and some other types of headaches, such as occipital and facial neuralgia (pressure on a nerve within the head), temporal arteritis (inflammation of the temporal artery) and cluster headaches (groups of intense one-sided headaches). People diagnosed with these other forms of headache may have accompanying tension headaches that can be helped with a manual therapy approach.

The origin of pre-menstrual headache has not been established. Both the tissues supporting the head and venous congestion may be responsible, since both are affected by changing hormonal levels. Indeed, mechanical factors might contribute to many symptoms of premenstrual tension, including backache, headache, fatigue, depression and lower abdominal pain.

A virulent infection, meningitis and myalgic encephalomyelitis (chronic fatigue syndrome) can leave muscular tension and upper neck stiffness long after the infection has disappeared. These residual headaches often have a mechanical basis and respond to manual therapy.

Some people have such a remarkable susceptibility to headache that the slightest provocation can produce it. Many of these, when examined, have upper neck stiffness and tension. They are excellent cases for manual therapy.

Some manual practitioners believe that certain head symptoms are due to mechanical disorders of the cranium itself. To treat these problems, practitioners of cranial manipulation and sacro-occipital technique apply their methods directly to the head. Exactly what they are, and how symptoms differ from those referred from the upper neck, has not been established. But there is little doubt that any pain, when referred from another site, responds more readily when gentle manual treatment is given to the area the pain has been referred to, as well as to its source.

Symptoms

Almost everyone will get a tension headache at some time. It can affect any part of the head and face except the lips, nose, chin and earflaps. The pain is felt as a dull, diffuse ache under the base of the skull, the forehead, the cheeks and at the side or on the top of the head. Unlike migraine, tension headaches are often bilateral, affecting both sides of the head.

The pain can be an awareness of discomfort, it can feel like a band around the head, a weight, a throbbing or pounding. There may be a feeling of fullness, pressure or stress in the head. It can feel like the pain is in or behind the eyes or in the cheeks. It sometimes comes with a feeling of tightly stretched facial skin or scalp, or with persistent twitching of a small muscle in the face or eyelid. Sometimes there are sharp immobilising jabs of pain. The ache can occur daily and last for hours, but it's rarely strong enough to take over a person's life.

Mechanism of pain

To manual practitioners, emotional fatigue or stress is not, as might be thought, the fundamental reason underlying tension headaches.

In some situations, it is true that the patient is living with a high level of stress, indicating there is a relationship. In other cases, there is noticeable stress, but it is not higher than at other times. Quite often, the person doesn't feel stressed at all and can feel quite indignant at the suggestion. Other people with high levels of stress and anxiety do not have headaches.

To manual practitioners, tension headaches are quite

straightforward. They all have one thing in common — tension of muscles attached under the base of the skull and restricted mobility of the upper neck joints.

The restricted mobility can be due to some recent physical or emotional fatigue. Often the origins are more long-standing, developing over weeks, months or years. It can come from holding the head and neck so that the muscles are under prolonged and continuous tension. The sustained low grade physical strain of typing, driving and assembly-line work are all capable of causing adaptive stiffness. There might be additional contributing factors such as aging and arthritis.

The restriction can result from a previous, sometimes forgotten, injury, such as a sporting collision, a household knock or a work strain, or a more memorable whiplash accident or other head trauma.

Once the restricted mobility exists, additional physical effort, tiring activity, fatigue or worry can tip the balance, causing you to suffer a series of headaches. Search your immediate past and you might find prolonged deskwork, job pressure, long car drives, too many late nights or general over-commitment.

Emotional pressure or fatigue might trigger a headache, but it is not usually the fundamental problem. The headache really depends on the degree of underlying neck trouble. A moderate but quiescent mechanical problem will require relatively low levels of stress to start a tension headache, so the complaint seems to be out of proportion to the cause. Sometimes the neck problem is sufficient that the headaches apparently come and go for no reason.

Treatment

Most tension headaches are annoying but tolerable. Self-help and avoidance of known causes are the usual forms of treatment. You could take paracetamol or an aspirin, do some simple neck-stretching exercises or ask a friend to massage your neck and scalp. You could lie down and enjoy your favourite tipple before having a hot shower or bath and an early night.

If the headache persists without obvious cause, and does not respond to self-help, see your doctor. The doctor's main role is to reach a diagnosis and treat serious causes of headache. Most often this will establish that there is nothing seriously wrong. We are left with the label 'tension headache' and advice about taking it easy or taking a long hard look at our lives. Sometimes identification and resolution of emotional problems or anxiety may be necessary.

If it is clear, and it often is, that you have tension headaches, then manual therapy is an ideal means of treating the problem and can bring wonderful immediate relief. It will complement medical advice, resolve muscular tension and neck stiffness and provide you with sustained relief from tension headaches, as well as reducing the need for medication.

Once the underlying mechanical disorder is resolved, your lifestyle should not cause headaches, even when you put the pressure back on. Relief from tension headaches is one of the great successes of manual therapy.

Vertigo

Vertigo, often described as giddiness or dizziness, gives a person the illusion that their surroundings are moving or spinning. It might be felt as a sense of falling, lightheadedness, unsteadiness, imbalance, or a feeling that the ground is moving.

Identifying the cause can be difficult and some forms of vertigo can be difficult to treat, even when the cause is known.

Mechanical causes

Vertigo may be due to an inner ear problem such as labyrinthitis, an infection, or Meniere's disease. However, the most common cause of vertigo is not in the ear at all. The most frequent culprit is aging in the neck. There are two distinct types: cervical vertigo and vertebrobasilar insufficiency.

Cervical vertigo is the most common form of vertigo; it is due to over-stimulation of the proprioceptive (balance and equilibrium) nerves in the neck. It occurs on certain head movements or positions, such as turning over in bed, and can be accompanied by neck pain, chronic muscle tension and joint stiffness. An X-ray might show arthritis.

Vertebrobasilar insufficiency is much less frequent and affects people in later life. In its mild form there is a feeling of faintness and unsteadiness when looking up, such as when hanging out the washing or watching something in the sky, or straining to look over the shoulder. The problem is caused by reduced blood flow in the two arteries (the vertebral arteries) that pass up to the brain through holes in the vertebrae of the neck. They become distorted and partially blocked with age. At the extremes of neck movement they are stretched and squeezed, reducing the flow of blood to the brain, and causing dizziness.

Manual practitioners have to be careful to distinguish between cervical vertigo and vertebrobasilar insufficiency. Although the neck causes both conditions, only the former can be helped by manual therapy, whereas occasionally it makes vertebrobasilar insufficiency worse.

Treatment

Medical treatment for cervical vertigo is to prescribe medication like Stemetil, and this is often helpful.

If the problem keeps recurring or there is accompanying

neck pain and stiffness, or you don't wish to take medication, manual therapy is highly effective. It works by reducing over-stimulation of the proprioceptive nerves (movement sensors) in the middle part of the neck. As well as relieving giddiness, manual therapy will also help any neck pain and stiffness that happens to be present at the same time.

For vertebrobasilar insufficiency there is no helpful medication or other treatment. Patients are simply recommended to avoid the extreme head positions that provoke dizziness.

NECK PAIN

- Acute torticollis
- Brachial neuritis
- Cervical ribs
- Whiplash

Refer to Chapter 11, General spinal disorders, for general conditions that affect the neck.

Acute torticollis

Acute torticollis (or wry neck) is a spasm of the neck muscles that develops overnight; it can be extremely painful.

The head is turned and bent sideways away from pain located in the upper neck. This condition, also called wry neck, is probably due to a sprained joint in the neck. Any attempt to straighten up is sharply painful. Sometimes an immobilising spasm can produce more damage. The problem usually develops in people when they are asleep. Occasionally it occurs when a person looks round over one shoulder or sits with their head turned for too long.

At night two factors combine: the person sleeps more soundly than normal and the neck lies in an uncomfortable position, perhaps having come off the pillow. Most sufferers recall that they slept heavily, often due to fatigue and sometimes alcohol. The pain that develops from the uncomfortable position does not disturb their sleep and they do not wake or turn to a new, more comfortable position. Body reflexes never go to sleep, so the painful position causes muscle spasm to develop. When the person finally wakes, the neck is all locked up. Any sort of movement is acutely painful. Muscle spasm on first stirring can even aggravate the injury.

Treatment

A minor case of torticollis usually wears off in one or two days. Rest, paracetamol, heat balm and a hot-water bottle might be all that are required. If it is more severe or persists for more than a couple of days, manual therapy, massage and ultrasound are helpful. Such treatment will speed recovery, minimise residual stiffness and reduce the possibility of future attacks.

Slower resolution or repeat episodes suggest that scar tissue and residual stiffness has already developed, creating an increased risk of future attacks. Here, manual therapy to relax muscle spasm and gently loosen the injured joint is necessary and gives good results.

Brachial neuritis

Brachial neuritis (also known as brachialgia) is pain accompanied by tingling and numbness, and sometimes muscle weakness in the arm and hand, due to pressure, injury or, rarely, infection of nerves in the brachial plexus (large nerves which pass from the neck down to supply the arm).

Causes

Conditions of the neck causing brachial neuritis include spondylosis, osteoarthritis, disc prolapse, whiplash injury, cervical rib and, rarely, tumour or infection.

Trauma to the brachial plexus is uncommon; it can occur through forcible falls onto the shoulder, as in a motorcycle accident. It can also be caused during birth.

Treatment

Treatment depends on the cause, extent and severity of nerve damage. Investigations may include X-ray and nerve conduction study, or myelography (X-ray examination of the spinal cord after injection of a contrast medium), CT (computer tomography) scan and MRI (magnetic resonance imaging) if surgery is contemplated.

Manual therapy can help osteoarthritis, spondylosis, prolapsed disc, whiplash and cervical rib — all described in this book. Tumour, infection and acute trauma require medical attention.

Cervical ribs

Cervical ribs (also known as thoracic outlet syndrome and scalenous syndrome) is where an extra pair of ribs has grown, on the lowest neck (cervical) vertebra, parallel to and immediately above the normal first ribs.

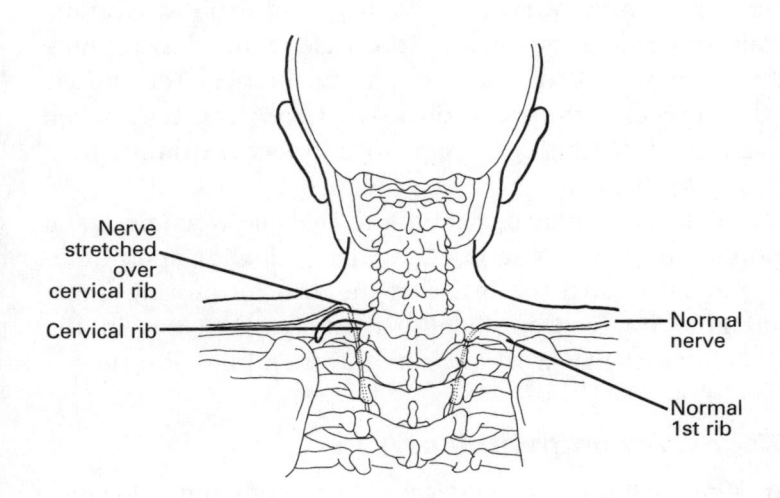

The back of the spine showing a cervical rib and scalene muscles

Types

Some people are born with cervical ribs. The abnormality can vary from a small bony protrusion to a fully formed rib and can occur on one or both sides. Occasionally there is a tough fibrous band in the place of a cervical rib.

Thoracic outlet syndrome (spasm of the scalene muscles at the side of the neck), also called scalenous syndrome, has exactly the same symptoms as cervical rib. Here, the normal first ribs are the cause of the problem.

Symptoms

Most people with cervical ribs live their lives without knowing about them, as they cause no symptoms. The extra ribs are discovered only when X-rays are taken for some other reason.

When an extra rib does become a problem, nerves become stretched over the top of the rib. Repetitive, forceful or prolonged use of the shoulders through activities such as running, sawing, carrying heavy bags and window cleaning leads to spasm of the muscles (the scalene muscles) running down the side of the neck to the upper ribs. The muscle spasm prevents the extra rib from descending fully when breathing out, causing tension to the nerves running over the top of them.

Initially there may be pain in the angle between neck and shoulder near the extra rib. Later, pain, tingling and numbness extend down the inside of the arm to the ring finger and little finger. Occasionally, weakness develops in the small muscles that work the ring finger and little finger.

Diagnosis and treatment

An X-ray will show if a cervical rib is present and help eliminate other causes of pain and tingling in the arm, such as disc degeneration and arthritis.

Manipulative practitioners believe most cases of cervical rib can be resolved with manual therapy. After all, the patient has had the extra rib for a lifetime without symptoms. The culprit is really spasm of the scalene muscles at the side of the neck. Manual therapy relaxes the muscles and frees up stiff joints in the upper neck and upper ribs where the muscles attach.

Medical treatment includes analgesic medication (painkillers), and rest and exercises to help relax the scalene muscles. If the problem remains or recurs it may be recommended that you have an operation to remove the offending rib. Manual therapy should always be tried first, as it is usually successful.

Whiplash

Whiplash (also known as acceleration–deceleration injury of the neck and cervical sprain) is a sprain of the soft tissues (muscle, ligament, joint capsule and disc) in the neck. In whiplash injuries, damage to the bones is rare.

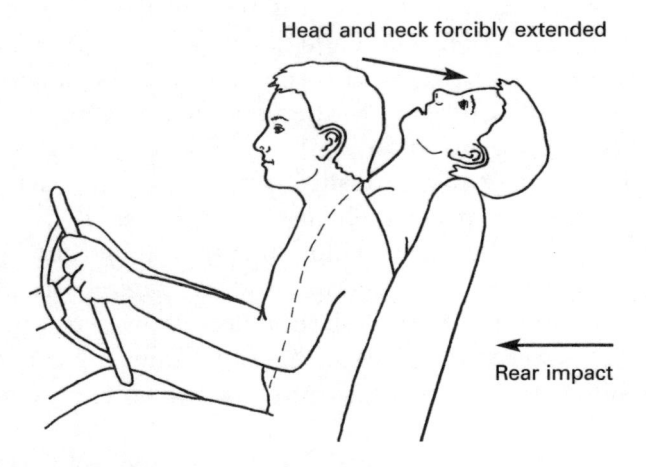

Whiplash injury

Whiplash commonly happens when a stationary car is hit from behind by another car. While the head stays still, the seat suddenly jerks the body forward. The front of the neck is injured as the neck is forcibly bent backward. In front-end collisions, the head continues forward while the body is suddenly stopped by the seat belt. Here, damage is done to the back of the neck and, if the head rebounds back, to the front of the neck. The damage can be worse if the head is turned at the time of impact or if the car is hit from the side. The introduction of front and side airbags in cars will help reduce the severity of some of these injuries.

Head restraints are useful in rear-end collisions because they carry the head forward with the body. They are less useful in front-end accidents. But because the posterior neck muscles are much stronger they give the neck some protection.

Symptoms

Often there are few symptoms immediately after the accident. However, the next day, the person wakes with an intensely stiff neck with pain spreading across the shoulders and sometimes into the chest and down the arms. They may be suffering from be a headache, sometimes accompanied by dizziness, tinnitus (ringing in the ears) and tingling in the arms. Use of the arms in any sort of prolonged or repetitive manner, such as carrying dishes, washing up or vacuum cleaning, only aggravates the pain.

The main problem with whiplash is that numerous neck joints and muscles and sometimes discs are injured. It's as if all the joints and muscles of the shoulder, elbow, wrist, hand and fingers were strained all at the same time. A pre-existing condition such as arthritis can make the problem worse and prolong the recovery.

Part of the trouble with whiplash comes from its invisibility. It is a soft tissue problem and firm pathological evidence is often lacking, with X-rays usually normal for the person's age.

Treatment

Initial treatment is to rest the neck. Temporary immobilisation in a cervical (neck) collar can be helpful, while anti-inflammatory analgesics (aspirin-like medication) will reduce pain and inflammation. Other treatments include heat, ultrasound and intermittent traction. As recovery begins, a manual practitioner may use massage and a graded introduction to other manual techniques and exercises.

The great majority of whiplash injuries recover complete pain-free mobility, although previous neck trouble or arthritis can slow recovery. Less often, whiplash results in chronic recurring bouts of symptoms. Many of these result from scar tissue and stiffness and respond well to manual therapy.

THE THORACIC SPINE AND CHEST

CHAPTER FOURTEEN

- Abdominal functional disturbance
- Chest wall pain ■ Heavy arm syndrome (T3 Syndrome) ■ Oesophageal (gullet) pain
- Respiratory restriction ■ Scheuermann's disease

Refer to Chapter 11, General spinal disorders, for general conditions that affect the thoracic spine.

Abdominal functional disturbance

(See Chapter 3, Functional disorders)
Abdominal functional disturbance refers to persistent abdominal flatulence (fullness or swelling of the bowels by gases formed during digestion), accompanied by indigestion and vaguely unpleasant sensations of discomfort, nausea, heartburn, acidity and appetite disturbance.

Causes

Flatulence and indigestion are symptoms, not diseases. They accompany numerous medical conditions such as gastritis, ulcer, appendicitis, gallstones, pregnancy, colitis, irritable bowel syndrome, bowel obstruction and tumour. While a medical practitioner might well find an organic disease (abnormal changes in tissues and cells), a functional disturbance is extremely common.

Functional problems include emotional causes (worry, anxiety states, exhaustion and stress), dietetic causes (unsuitable food, hasty meals, over- and under-eating) and, in the opinion of osteopaths and chiropractors, mechanical causes (referred pain and reflexes).

If severe pain or weight loss are prominent, the condition is probably an organ disease. If these are absent and there is fatigue, tension, stiffness or discomfort between the shoulder blades, if the abdominal problem keeps recurring or has persisted for some time without progressing, it is more likely to be a functional disorder.

> William, aged 32, is an analyst for a bank and spends long hours in front of the computer. He presented to his doctor with an abdominal disturbance. He had a sense of fullness and bloating, with mild nausea and indigestion, and sometimes just a general sense of discomfort, particularly when he was over-tired. He had to loosen his belt a notch and his trousers always seemed to feel tight. There was no consistent pattern to point strongly towards a diagnosis, and although the doctor suspected nerves were at the bottom of it, he discussed the possibility of irritable bowel syndrome, an ulcer and gallstones. Medication was prescribed, partly as a diagnostic test, but it made no difference.
>
> As the problem was not improving, the doctor referred William for a specialist's opinion, but further tests failed to show any problem. After numerous investigations, including blood tests and a colonoscopy, the condition was finally labelled a functional disorder. This is one way of saying Something is definitely wrong but nothing seems to be the matter. Sometimes the term is used to imply it's in your head. A doctor will talk about stress, anxiety and nerves. In William's case, he left the practice with a prescription for antispasmodic and sedative medication, and advice about easing up on his lifestyle, taking regular holidays and doing exercise.

Some patients might accept this state of affairs. They have been given a firm label and they have a bottle of tablets. Besides, the symptoms do feel worse when they are stressed and tired and they improve with a few early nights and some exercise. They might think the complaint is 'just part of getting older', since we all expect to deteriorate in vague ways as we age.

William was one of those cases where conventional medicine failed to recognise the value of manual therapy. He was told: 'There is nothing to worry about, you worry too much and there's nothing wrong'. But the symptoms were still disturbing and interfered with his work and the enjoyment of life. Also, William felt he was not a worrier, and his wife and friends all scoffed at the idea. Surely the doctor was barking up the wrong tree.

William came to see me because he had consulted a naturopath about his digestive problem and was told that he might have something wrong with his back. It was a roundabout route, but finally William was on the right track.

Patients do not find the problem trivial and manual therapy might provide a simple cure. The digestive tract is essentially a muscular organ, which is quite capable of developing referred pain and reflexes that interfere with normal function.

Although osteopaths and chiropractors have little hard scientific evidence other than numerous anecdotal successes during 100 years of experience, they believe the thoracic spine is an unrecognised cause of abdominal malfunction.

Symptoms and diagnosis

The most common symptom is a persistently full, bloated or swollen abdomen, which is intermittent but can last for days. Low- to medium-grade discomfort may be present in any part of the abdomen, centrally, on one or both sides, or in the kidney region, groin or testicles. It can feel surprisingly like a disease. It can feel nauseous, queasy, sharp, cramping, aching, burning, pulling, throbbing and heavy. There may be loose bowels, constipation, dysmenorrhoea (painful periods) and increased frequency of passing water.

A mechanical disorder should be considered when symptoms do not fit well with a real organ disease. They are weak and not as pronounced as they should be, are present when they should not be, and do not respond to medication designed to treat the suspected organ problem. Like all mechanical problems, it is also worse with fatigue and stress, and responds to rest, exercise and muscle-relaxing tablets.

The patient might have discomfort, tightness or stiffness between the shoulder blades, poor posture or previous episodes of pain between the shoulder blades. However, the back may be without symptoms and not draw any attention to itself.

On examination, patients have muscular tension and joint stiffness in the middle back, about level with the lower ends of the shoulder blades. This is the segmentally related part of the back that refers pain and reflexes to the abdomen. The back muscles are highly sensitive, noticeably hard and stringy with a fibrous texture, and the joints have a pronounced resistance to movement. The history and signs indicate a chronic (longstanding) back problem.

Some functional disorders require medical assessment before a competent manual practitioner might wish to give treatment. It might be necessary for specialised investigations to exclude an organ disease that requires medical treatment.

However, if the history supports it, and the back has sufficient muscular tension and joint stiffness in the correct location, we might start a short trial of three or four treatments. Like all cases with referred pain and reflexes, we treat the source of symptoms in the back and gently relax the muscular digestive tract to assist recovery.

Chest wall pain

Pain located around the rib cage to the side and front of the chest.

Causes

Sufferers of pain around the chest wall are frequently concerned that they have a serious medical disorder of the heart, lung or breast. Although one must always consider the possibility that the symptoms are of cardiac origin, the most common reason for chest wall pain in a person under 40 years of age is referred pain from the thoracic spine (upper back). After unaccustomed and prolonged looking down or physical effort, the upper back becomes fatigued, tense and stiff, and can refer pain around the chest wall. Computer work, deskwork, sewing, standing to work at a bench, pulling and pushing furniture, digging in the garden and motor accidents can all trigger chest wall pain.

There may be a previous history of intervertebral joint strain or muscle spasm in the area between the shoulder blades, costovertebral (joint between a rib and vertebra) sprain or Scheuermann's disease (a growth disorder of adolescent vertebra), which can all leave the back stiff.

If a physical cause is not obvious, further tests may be needed; a medical practitioner usually arranges these. Chest problems which need to be excluded include coronary artery disease, myocardial infarct (heart attack), chest infection, pleurisy, gall bladder disease, rib fracture, polymyalgia rheumatica and, rarely, secondary carcinoma in a rib. Breast tumours are rarely painful.

Symptoms

Pain referred from the thoracic spine (upper back) can affect any part of the chest wall. It may be felt in the axilla, at the side of the rib cage, in the midline over the sternum (breastbone), or within or behind a breast. It may be felt as a constant dull ache, a pressure or tightness lasting days, weeks or even months. An immobilising stab of pain lasting several seconds may be sufficient to prevent breathing (see Respiratory restriction p. 202). Chest wall pain can radiate into the arm and, when on the left side, can mimic angina (coronary artery disease) or a heart attack.

Other symptoms include tightness between the shoulder blades, which eases when they are squeezed together, and popping or clicking in the front of the ribs. Sometimes there is a mild burning sensation behind the sternum as food becomes caught as it passes down the oesophagus (see Oesophageal pain, p. 201); at other times there might be heaviness, pain and tingling in the arm (see Heavy arm syndrome, p. 200).

Diagnosis and treatment

On examination there is muscular tension and tenderness of the intercostal (between two ribs) muscles in the area of pain. The part of the back segmentally related (connected) to the chest pain has pronounced muscle spasm and joint stiffness and is highly tender. With careful probing, people are quick to realise that the source of the problem has been located in their back. X-ray of the thoracic spine is not usually needed as it usually adds little to the clinical picture.

It is mostly easy to distinguish between mechanical pain and heart pain, but it can require medical assessment.

The simplest test is to physically stress the chest wall without straining the heart. Take a big breath, twist left and right, take your head to your knees and then look at the ceiling. If any of these movements increase the pain, it is likely to be mechanical. Angina (heart pain), on the other hand, does not change with physical position. There is usually a graded onset of pain as the heart rate increases, such as when walking up a slope or steps. Angina patients also experience breathlessness, sweating, nausea and belching. They tend to be a little older and there may be cardiac risk factors, such as a family history, obesity and smoking.

For suspected medical problems such as heart disease, gall bladder disease, carcinoma, polymyalgia rheumatica and pleurisy, further tests may need to be organised by your medical practitioner.

Immediate measures for chest wall pain coming from the back include pain-killers, lying or sitting down with a hot-water bottle, or even a cold pack, and gentle massage using a heat rub. This is best applied between the shoulder blades but can help when applied directly to the source of the pain.

If the pain continues, manual therapy is most helpful. It is generally applied to the source of the trouble in the back. Referred pain usually indicates a more longstanding problem, so the back may require several treatments for sustained recovery. Gentle but deep massage is an important element. Other treatments include heat, ultrasound, exercises and anti-inflammatory drugs.

Heavy arm syndrome (T3 syndrome)

Heavy arm syndrome, sometimes known as T3 syndrome, has no clear identity in medical texts, yet it is a common condition that responds well to manual therapy. The syndrome (group of symptoms and signs) is due to a strain of the third thoracic (T3) segment in the upper back. It possibly causes symptoms via the autonomic (involuntary) nervous system. Usually it affects one arm but it can develop in both.

During the day the main complaint is a curious sense of heaviness, weakness or fatigue of the arm, accompanied by a weak handgrip. It is an effort to lift the arm and grip, for example when hanging out washing and squeezing pegs, or when using the arm repetitively in motions such as brushing hair or vacuuming. Muscular tightness or aching may be felt between the shoulder blades.

Other symptoms include tingling of the hand, puffiness or swelling of the fingers and a sense of stiffness in the fingers. There may be pain in the back of the upper arm, sometimes diffusely affecting the whole arm. These symptoms are most pronounced on waking, but they can persist throughout the day.

The disorder often starts when the person is fatigued by unaccustomed or prolonged sitting with the head in a fixed position, such as when writing, typing, working at a computer, driving, sewing or working at a bench. When the patient is examined, there is marked tenderness and spasm, with fibrotic hard muscles and stiffness centred on the joint between the third and fourth thoracic vertebrae.

The arm symptoms are somewhat similar to carpal tunnel syndrome (a trapped nerve in the wrist). The patient sometimes needs an electrical test called a nerve conduction study to distinguish one from the other.

Manual therapy is the treatment of choice for heavy arm syndrome. Although treatment is similar to that for chest wall pain, emphasis is given to the upper thoracic region, particularly to the third thoracic segment.

Oesophageal (gullet) pain

This refers to swallowing discomfort in the oesophagus (the muscular tube joining the throat to the stomach) behind the sternum (breastbone) due to a mechanical problem in the upper thoracic spine.

This less common functional disorder gives a sensation of pressure, burning or pain behind the breastbone and a feeling of food catching in the oesophagus on its way down to the stomach. It may require a second or third swallow to push the food past the sense of stricture and there might be slight to moderate discomfort at the point of catching.

A mechanical disorder in the upper back should be suspected when the problem is mild, keeps recurring with a variable intensity and is accompanied by fatigue, tightness or discomfort between the shoulder blades. If a mechanical problem is not obvious or there is no improvement after one or two treatments, medical referral for further tests might be required.

Respiratory restriction

The symptoms of this common breathing problem are a sensation of restricted inspiration and chest tightness. It may be accompanied by pain in the back, between the shoulder blades or around the chest wall.

When mild, there is a sense of restricted inspiration. In more severe cases, the sufferer finds that expiration (breathing out) is also restricted, giving them a sense of shallow breathing, an inability to get enough air or even suffocation. Chest wall and back pain may develop as the problem becomes more marked.

Sometimes a sudden, quite severe stab of pain that prevents breathing for several seconds is felt. Occasionally the distress is so great as to make the patient quite afraid to breathe.

On examination, a manual practitioner will find thoracic spasm, tenderness and restricted intervertebral mobility similar to that for chest wall pain. Manual treatment is equally effective.

Scheuermann's disease

Scheuermann's disease (also known as adolescent kyphosis, rounded back and osteochondritis) is named after the German physician who first described it. It is a common disorder of the thoracic spine (upper back). It occurs in about 20 per cent of adolescents between the ages of 11 and 18, and affects boys slightly more than girls. Some of the thoracic vertebrae become wedge-shaped and the discs between them become thinner. This leads to a 'kyphosis' or rounded upper back, stiffness and sometimes backache. After the condition has healed, as it always does, the rounded posture and X-ray appearance of Scheuermann's disease remain for the rest of a person's life.

Symptoms and signs

Scheuermann's disease usually has few symptoms. More frequently, an adolescent child will complain of mild backache after sport, physical effort and lifting strains. Parents may put it down to 'growing pains', but those who notice a stooped posture or a stiff back in their teenage children should seek advice, particularly if their child complains of backache.

Those who have evidence of Scheuermann's disease tend to suffer from slightly increased backache as adults. Back pain in adult life is sometimes diagnosed as Scheuermann's disease, even though it has long since healed. In this case, the pain is usually due to strain or minor injury to the stiff region. Later, spondylosis (degeneration) may develop in the same region and lead to backache.

Treatment

Treatment is recommended for those who complain of pain. Some people believe it also assists those who have a rounded back and stiffness but no pain. They say that the back is less likely to give trouble in the future if the stiffness is reduced.

Young people with Scheuermann's disease are recommended to avoid the sports and physical activities that cause symptoms. Exercises are given to improve mobility and help prevent an increase in back roundedness, but they cannot correct an existing deformity. Gentle manual therapy will relieve pain, ease muscular tension and improve flexibility.

Manual practitioners believe these measures may help prevent future back pain and reduce the development of degenerative changes.

THE LOWER BACK

CHAPTER FIFTEEN

- Coccydinia
- Sacroiliac joint strain
- Sciatica
- Spondylolysis
- Spondylolisthesis

Refer to Chapter 11, General spinal disorders, for general conditions that affect the lower back.

Coccydinia

Coccydinia is a painful and tender coccyx or tailbone which prevents a person from sitting comfortably. The coccyx is a group of four or five small bones at the base of the spine — all that remain of our evolutionary ancestor's tail.

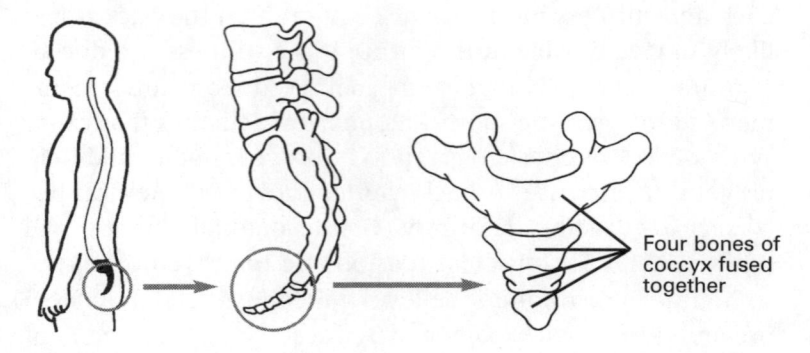

Four bones of coccyx fused together

The location of the coccyx

Causes

There are two types of coccydynia: the first and most frequent arises from a mechanical problem in the lower back; the second results from direct injury to the coccyx.

The lower back variety generates pain in the coccyx by painful spasm of a muscle, the gluteus maximus, attaching to the coccyx. The direct injury pain might be caused by a fall onto the coccyx, such as sitting down without a chair being there. Alternatively, it can be caused by pressure from sitting slouched in a hard chair for too long or the passage of a baby at childbirth.

There is a simple test to see whether you have a back problem causing coccyx pain or a direct injury to the coccyx. Sit on a chair, concentrate on the area in question and start to stand up. A mechanical back problem will immediately aggravate the coccyx pain because the gluteus maximus (buttock muscle) contracts very strongly in order to stand up, and this is painful. An injured coccyx immediately feels better, since you are no long sitting on the injury.

The same thing happens in reverse as you sit down. The back problem gives coccyx pain during the process of becoming seated, when the gluteus maximus muscle is contracting most strongly, and is immediately eased upon sitting. A bony injury is not painful until you have sat down and placed pressure on the tender tail bone.

Treatment

If the source of the coccydynia is the back, a manual practitioner will find muscle spasm, joint stiffness and tenderness in the lower back with spasm of the muscles attaching to the coccyx. In this case, manual therapy to the back and buttock muscle will solve the problem.

When the problem is caused by a bony injury, sitting on a blow-up ring or using two cushions to relieve pressure is the main treatment. If progress is slow, an injection of local anaesthetic and cortisone can be effective.

Sacroiliac joint strain

This is strain of one of a pair of joints joining the sacrum (the triangular bone at the base of the spine) to each ilium (the large bones on each side of the pelvis). Symptoms include pain in the region of the sacroiliac joint, with pain referred into the buttock and posterior thigh.

The existence of sacroiliac strain has caused debate ever since osteopaths and chiropractors first described it over a century ago. There is still no firm consensus on the matter.

The joints are large, with snugly fitting surfaces held in place by exceptionally powerful ligaments that permit only minimal movement. Orthodox practitioners feel that they are near impossible to strain, and lump sacroiliac strain in with the tooth fairy.

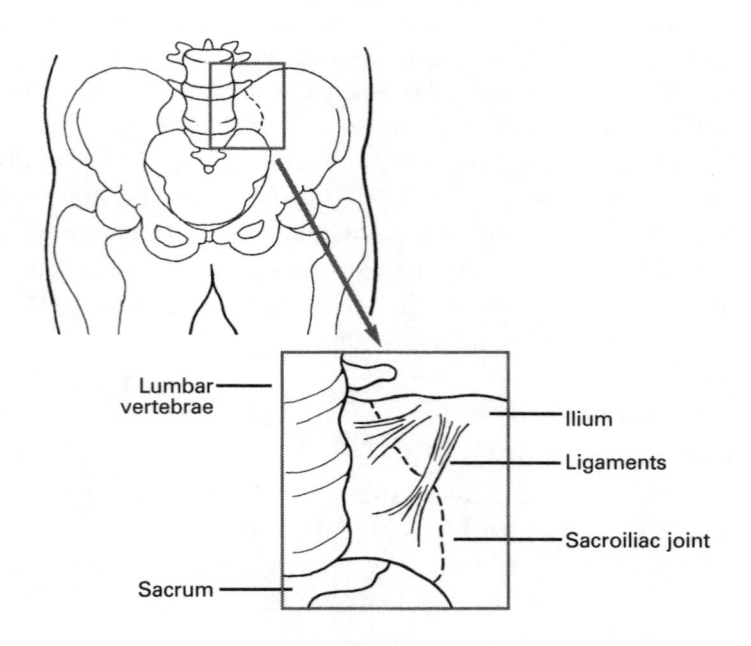

The location of the sacroiliac joint

In contrast, osteopaths and chiropractors have built the condition into a whole family of complaints with numerous symptoms and signs. Gradually, orthodox medicine has conceded that sacroiliac joint movement does occur and the joint can be strained, but only as result of trauma, strenuous physical activity, or perhaps childbirth. At the same time, osteopaths and chiropractors are becoming less sure of themselves and diagnose sacroiliac strain less often, preferring to blame 'sacroiliac symptoms' on the lower back.

Some will say they can manipulate the sacroiliac joint to relieve a group of symptoms and signs believed to arise from it. Others say that the small movements of the joint cannot be felt accurately or specifically tested, the joint cannot be manipulated, and treatment aimed at it works instead on the joints of the lower back.

One thing we can be sure of, the confusion means that no one has the right to be over-confident. Whether or not your practitioner believes sacroiliac strains occur rarely or frequently is not so important in the end. The group of lower back and pelvic symptoms which carry the name 'sacroiliac strain' are successfully treated with a manual therapy approach, whether or not it works on the sacroiliac or lower back joints.

Sciatica

Sciatica is pain down the back of the leg along the sciatic nerve. Pain is felt in the buttock, thigh, calf and foot. In severe cases, the pain may be accompanied by tingling, numbness and muscle weakness. Reflexes tested with a patella hammer become reduced or disappear.

The sciatic nerve is the main nerve in each leg. It supplies the hip joint and the skin and muscles behind the thigh; below the knee the nerve supplies all of the muscles, joints and skin.

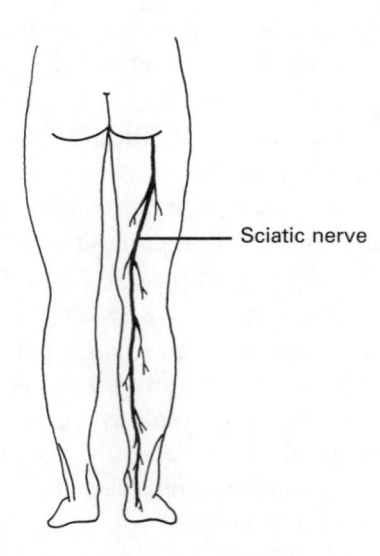

Sciatic nerve pathway

Types and causes

Three types of back problem can cause pain in the leg. All of them might be described as 'sciatica' simply because the lower back is the source of the pain, but only one is true sciatica.

True sciatica is due to irritation of the sciatic nerve, usually by pressure from a prolapsed disc pressing on the sciatic nerve root in the back (see Chapter 3, Trapped nerves). Sometimes simply sitting in an awkward position or on a badly designed seat can cause temporary sciatica. Less often, an arthritic bony spur (outgrowth) or spinal stenosis (narrowing of the spinal canal) compresses the sciatic nerve. Rarely, a tumour, infection, alcoholism or diabetes can cause sciatica.

Femoral nerve irritation is similar to sciatica but it affects the femoral nerve in the front of the thigh. Femoral nerve irritation has the same causes as true sciatica. It occurs less frequently because the femoral nerve starts higher up the back where prolapsed discs are less common.

Referred pain to the leg from the lower back is often mistakenly called sciatica (see Chapter 3, Referred pain). Referred pain is a deep diffuse ache that rarely travels further than the knee and there is no tingling, numbness, muscle weakness or reflex changes.

Treatment

Sciatica is a symptom and not a disease; in each case, treatment is given to the underlying cause.

The advice and treatment from a manual practitioner is a great help for the usual causes: a prolapsed disc and degeneration. As well as gentle manual therapy, measures might include temporary rest in bed, heat packs, mobilising exercises and anti-inflammatory analgesics (aspirin-like drugs). Referred pain to the leg from a strained back is much less fearsome. Manual therapy is usually the best treatment.

If pressure on the sciatic nerve is marked, an epidural injection may be needed. This is a method of pain relief in which local anaesthetic is injected into the epidural space in the lower back to numb the sciatic nerve. In rare cases surgery may be needed for large disc prolapse, spinal stenosis or tumour.

Spondylolysis

Spondylolysis is a disorder of the spine in which a stress fracture (a fracture without obvious trauma) develops in the fifth, or rarely the fourth, lumbar (lower back) vertebra and does not reunite. A bridge of fibrous tissue makes a strong connection between the two bony pieces. Although not usually a problem, it can be seen on X-ray for the rest of the person's life.

Spondylolysis develops in about 4 per cent of people between the ages of 18 and 22. Athletes who lean backwards a lot are particularly at risk. These include fast bowlers, gymnasts, weightlifters, rugby players and rowers. Sometimes the fracture line of a spondylolysis opens up, leading to a spondylolisthesis (forward slippage of one vertebra on the one below).

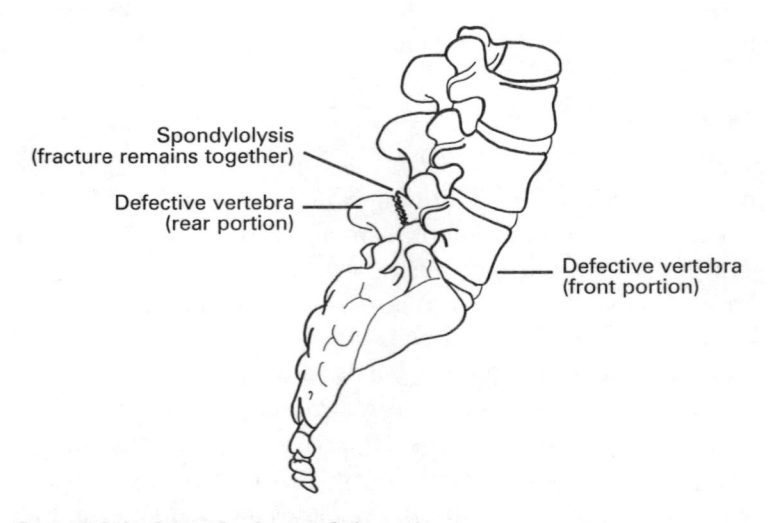

Spondylolysis at the base of the spine

Symptoms and treatment

A spondylolysis is usually seen years after the initial injury, when the two bony pieces are strongly united by fibrous tissue and the spondylolysis is not the cause of symptoms. When discovered, spondylolysis is a coincidental finding. The spondylolysis indicates only that the back has suffered previous heavy stresses. Pain might be due to sprain of a nearby joint, possibly made stiff by the person's earlier physical lifestyle.

If there is evidence that the stress fracture is recent on a bone scan (a method of checking for fractures) in a young adult, some rest may be necessary, and the patient may be advised to avoid playing sport. However, most spondylolyses are old and symptomless, and treatment is directed to the real cause of pain, perhaps sprain of an adjacent joint.

Manual therapy can focus treatment to the problem joint, most often the lowest spinal joint. Other treatment may include anti-inflammatory drugs, ultrasound and exercises.

Spondylolisthesis

This is a disorder of the spine in which one vertebra (spinal bone) slips forward on the one below. A slippage of the lowest lumbar vertebra on the sacrum (a triangular bone at the base of the spine forming part of the pelvis) is the most common.

Causes

Spondylolisthesis usually develops from a spondylolysis (a vertebral stress fracture that does not unite). Physical activity slowly stretches the fibrous bridge of scar tissue connecting the two non-united bony pieces of a spondylolysis and allows slippage to occur. In elderly people, one vertebra can slip on another due to arthritic wear and slack ligaments.

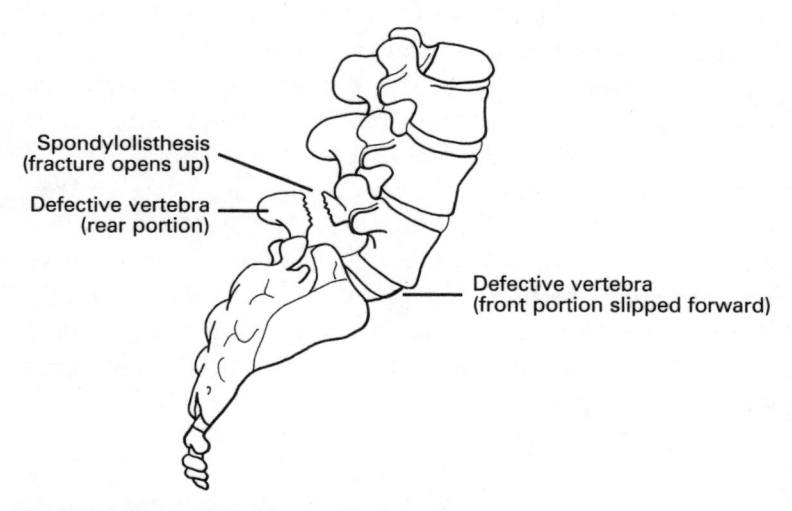

Spondylolisthesis at the base of the spine

Symptoms and signs

Spondylolisthesis is suspected when a step-like bony lump is seen in the midline of the lower back and confirmed by X-rays of the spine.

The problem might be 'stable', with little or no movement between the two bony pieces, or 'unstable' when the two bony pieces move relative to each other. Instability is likely when the fibrous bridge is more stretched and there is a greater gap between the two bony pieces with more slippage.

A stable spondylolisthesis is more common and causes less trouble. Like spondylolysis, it is old evidence of heavy stresses previously placed on the back. Backache then results from strain of a nearby joint, possibly made stiff by the physical stresses that caused the fracture years earlier.

An unstable spondylolisthesis can be more troublesome, with pain during physical activity and sometimes sciatica.

Treatment

A stable spondylolisthesis can be treated like a chronic back strain. Manual therapy helps relax and loosen muscles, ligaments and joints, which are the cause of symptoms. Other treatment might include anti-inflammatory drugs, heat, ultrasound and exercises.

An unstable spondylolisthesis needs more care to treat the troublesome stiff joint immediately below the two unstable and mobile pieces of vertebra. Manual treatment is gentle, usually without manipulation. Sometimes, when the vertebra slips too far, a spondylolisthesis can cause sciatica. Rarely, an operation to fuse the affected vertebra may become necessary.

CHAPTER SIXTEEN

ARM PAIN

- Acromio-clavicular (AC) joint strain
- Bursitis ■ Finger sprain ■ Fracture and dislocation ■ Frozen shoulder ■ Golfer's elbow ■ Shoulder pain ■ Tendinitis
- Tennis elbow ■ Tenosynovitis ■ Thumb pain ■ Wrist sprain

Acromio-clavicular (AC) joint strain

The acromio-clavicular or A/C joint lies between the outer end of the clavicle (collarbone) and the acromion (part of the shoulder blade at the tip of the shoulder).

A fall onto the shoulder can result in sprain, partial dislocation or, occasionally, complete dislocation. Body contact sports such as soccer, rugby and AFL, as well as horse riding and motorcycle accidents are common causes of injury.

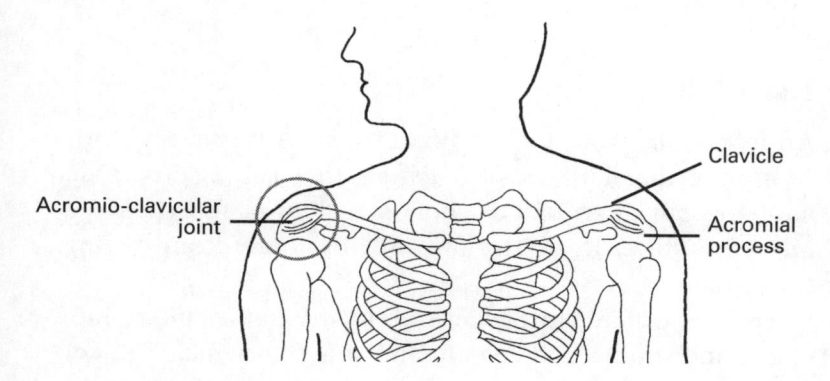

The location of the acromio-clavicular joint

In a simple sprain, there is swelling, pain, tenderness and restricted movement. In partial dislocation, the ligaments are stretched, there is greater swelling and the bones are slightly misaligned. In dislocation, ligaments joining the clavicle to the shoulder blade are ruptured and the bones are completely misaligned. Pain, tenderness and restriction of movement are pronounced.

Treatment of sprain consists of rest and application of icepacks several times daily. The pain and swelling usually settles down within a few days. Partial dislocation might require the arm and shoulder to be rested in a sling. An injection of local anaesthetic and cortisone can help speed up recovery when the pain is not settling. A permanent residual lump or 'step' deformity might remain. Dislocation always leaves an unsightly permanent lump unless reduced in a special splint (Kenny-Howard splint) for six weeks. Occasionally surgery might be needed to re-align the two halves of the joint.

A residual lump can often be seen after acromio-clavicular injury, but it usually gives little trouble. Partial and complete dislocation does not normally prevent a return to active sport. Persistent pain can be effectively helped with manual therapy and exercises. Sometimes a cortisone injection is needed.

Bursitis

An inflamed, swollen and painful bursa. A bursa is a lubricating sac that lies between tissues that rub against each another. It is often found where a tendon or muscle slides around a bone. The bursa prevents the bone from fraying the tendon or muscle.

The important bursae lie around the ankle, knee, hip, elbow and shoulder. Prepatellar bursitis (housemaid's knee) is caused by prolonged kneeling, while olecranon bursitis (student's elbow) is due to pressure of the elbow against a desktop. Subacromial bursitis, under the tip of the shoulder, may be due to unaccustomed overhead activity.

On the outside, widest part of the hip a painful area can develop which is known as trochanteric bursitis. Medical treatment is by injection with cortisone, but the problem tends to return. Manipulative practitioners believe that a mechanical disorder in the lower back is responsible for many of these cases.

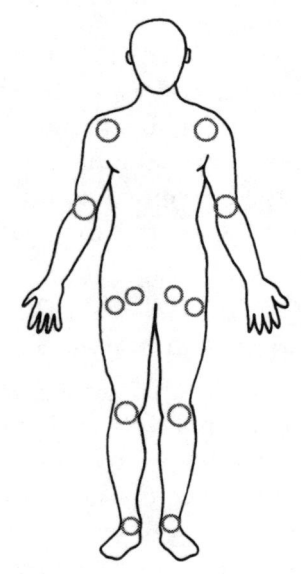

Common sites of bursitis

Treatment

Manual therapy is most helpful to reduce muscle spasm, congestion and pressure irritation, particularly when recovery is slow or the bursitis recurs. Application of an icepack can assist fluid to subside and reduce pain. Rest and anti-inflammatory medication is helpful.

Sometimes the bursa may be drained by a medical practitioner using a needle and syringe, or injected with cortisone to reduce the inflammation. If the bursitis on the outside of the hip does not respond to injection or recurs, more sustained recovery might be possible with manual therapy.

Finger sprain

Injuries to the fingers are common, particularly during ball games and among manual workers. Mallet finger is a rupture of the tendon where it attaches to the back of the finger following a blow to the fingertip. An X-ray may be required to exclude a fracture.

Sprain of a finger can be slow to recover. Early and repeated use of ice or iced water will help reduce swelling. If pain and stiffness persist, manual therapy, ultrasound, home massage and mobilising (loosening) techniques will help recovery. A mallet finger requires splinting with the finger straight for eight weeks so that the tendon can re-attach itself.

Fracture and dislocation

Fracture and dislocation are medical problems that are not managed by manual practitioners, except when given as first aid. However, a fracture nearly always damages surrounding muscles and ligaments, which can cause persistent scar tissue and more long-term problems than the fracture itself.

Lengthy immobilisation for fractures can lead to scar tissue with joint stiffness and pain long after the bone has repaired. If this is the case, a patient might think the fracture is the source of their pain, when overload and damage to scar tissue (fibrous bands of collagen left over after healing) is the real cause.

Dislocation can result in similar scar tissue, stiffness and pain months or years after an injury.

Treatment

Manual therapy is highly beneficial in the late treatment of persistent pain and stiffness after fracture and dislocation.

Manual therapy helps reduce adhesions and scar tissue. It restores the soft tissue extensibility and joint flexibility, which is essential for pain-free movements. Other physical therapy may include ultrasound and special mobilising exercises. Injection of local anaesthetic and cortisone can help when pain is localised to a small area.

It should be noted that 'subluxation' or 'misalignment' is not a minor degree of dislocation, as once believed. These terms, often used by chiropractors, refer to what conventional medicine calls a joint strain or, as in this book, a mechanical disorder.

Frozen shoulder

This common condition (also known as adhesive capsulitis) is unique to the shoulder joint. Stiffness usually develops for no apparent reason, caused by inflammation, adhesions and shrinkage in a large fold of the capsule (the loose membranous sac enclosing the joint) hanging below the shoulder joint. The shoulder has the most extensive loose capsule in the body to allow the joint great mobility. In severe cases, there is no movement of the joint at all and the pain is intense.

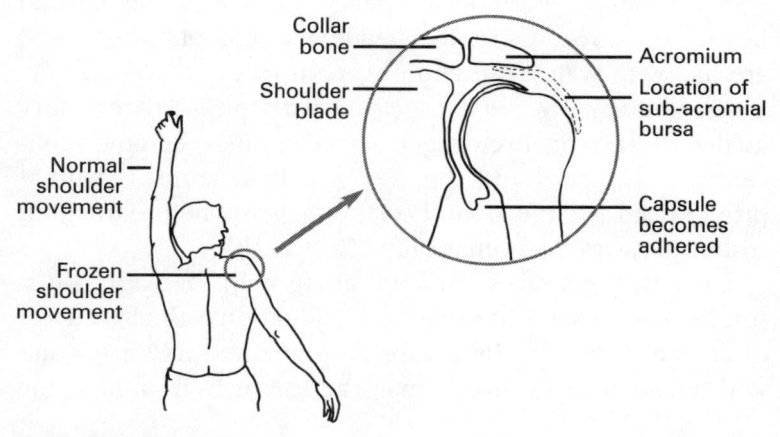

Frozen shoulder

Symptoms

A middle-aged person begins to feel a mild ache in the shoulder. Gradually, over three or four months the pain increases and spreads down the outside of the upper arm. The pain becomes constant and is worse at night. Limitation of movement is now clearly apparent.

Over the next three to four months, the pain eases but the joint remains 'frozen'. Six to eight months after the start, the pain has largely gone but the joint is still stiff. Mobility then gradually recovers over the next three or four months. The whole cycle takes from 9 to 15 months to complete.

Treatment

Twenty-five years ago, exercise and stretching of adhesions was recommended to restore movement, but we now know that this is counterproductive and only delays recovery. Ultimately, faster progress is achieved by resting the arm, allowing the painful phase to pass more quickly.

Spasm of the muscles around the shoulder causes pain. Here, massage and pendulum (swinging) exercises can help relax the muscles and ease some of the pain, but they will not shorten the overall recovery time.

Some people with lesser pain, when told the natural history of a frozen shoulder leading to complete recovery, are happy to wait it out without treatment.

Moderate pain can be helped with anti-inflammatory analgesics (aspirin-like drugs), gentle manual therapy, application of icepacks and the use of a heat lamp. If pain is pronounced, an injection of cortisone, given before the joint stiffens up, can be dramatically effective.

Once stiffness has set in and, along with the pain, is disturbing the person's lifestyle, hydrodilitation is the treatment of choice. Here, the joint capsule is inflated like a balloon with an injection of local anaesthetic, cortisone and saline solution. This procedure stretches out the adhering folds that prevent movement and can be highly effective. Patients leave pain-free and with greatly improved mobility.

Golfer's elbow

Golfer's elbow is another name for tendinitis on the inner part of the elbow and of the muscles which close the hand and bend the wrist down. It is caused by gripping and twisting activities such as using a hammer or screwdriver, or playing golf or tennis with a faulty grip or swing.

Treatment

If the problem is due to sport, it might be wise to rest the arm for a few weeks and seek the advice of a professional about playing technique. Treatment consists of manual therapy, application of icepacks and heat balms, wearing a tennis elbow cuff, ultrasound treatment and taking anti-inflammatory drugs. In severe or persistent cases, an injection of cortisone might be needed.

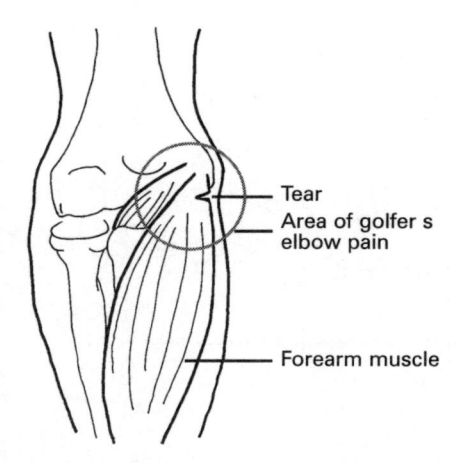

The location of golfer s elbow

Shoulder pain

Shoulder injuries are relatively common because the design favours mobility at the expense of strength and stability.

The shoulder can be affected by any of the disorders that affect the joints, including tendinitis (inflammation of a tendon), shoulder cuff syndrome (tendinitis of several tendons), ruptured tendon, bursitis (inflammation of a bursa), frozen shoulder (stiff and painful shoulder), sprain and dislocation. Osteoarthritis is unusual in the shoulder because it is a non-weight bearing joint.

Pain can also be referred to the shoulder from other places such as the neck, upper back, gall bladder, diaphragm, lungs and heart.

Treatment

It is necessary to distinguish shoulder conditions from pain referred to the shoulder. A manual practitioner can advise on and treat all the common shoulder disorders and most of the neck and upper back problems that refer pain to the shoulder.

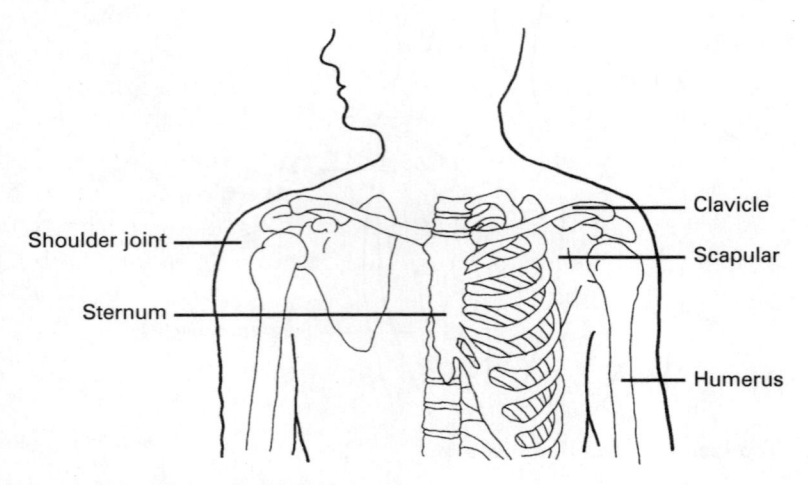

Components of the shoulder

More severely painful tendinitis, bursitis and frozen shoulder might need to be treated with an injection of local anaesthetic and cortisone, given by a medical practitioner. A ruptured tendon, such as the biceps or supraspinatous tendon, often causes surprisingly little disability and does not always warrant surgery.

Medical advice should be sought if there is a suspicion that symptoms are caused by pain referred from the heart, lungs or gall bladder.

Tendinitis

Tendinitis is inflammation of a tendon, usually caused by repetitive and unaccustomed overuse. It is one of the most common musculoskeletal injuries to the arms and legs.

Sporting pursuits are a common cause of tendinitis. Taking up a racket sport, such as tennis, or increasing the time spent playing can be responsible for wrist, elbow or shoulder tendinitis. Running activities can cause tendinitis in the knee or foot. Home maintenance tasks such as window cleaning, gardening, sawing and hammering can start the problem. Sometimes the cause can be as simple as returning to work from a holiday or changing occupation to a new activity.

Common sites of tendinitis include supraspinatous tendinitis (tip of the shoulder), rotator cuff syndrome (tendinitis of several shoulder tendons) and biceps tendinitis (front of the upper arm). Golf and tennis elbow are both forms of tendinitis associated with gripping. Achilles (back of the heel) and infra-patella (below the kneecap) tendinitis are both caused by running.

Symptoms, signs and treatment

Characteristically, tendinitis is first noticed as stiffness and pain sometime following exercise, often the next morning. There is pain on use, which can become less noticeable with continued use, only to return after exercise. Athletes report that they can 'run through' the pain or that the pain disappears when they warm up. On examination, the tendon is tender and sometimes swollen, with spasm in the muscle attached to the affected tendon.

A sprained tendon is slower to recover than a strained muscle because tendons receive significantly less blood supply. The blood supply to a tendon suffering from tendinitis is further reduced by reflex spasm of the attached muscle. Try stretching the skin on the back of one hand and you will notice the skin blanches and the blood vessels empty out. Recovery is delayed if the muscle attached to the tendon is in spasm 24 hours a day.

Soft tissue massage to relax the muscle belly is important to reduce tension in the tendon, assist its blood flow and promote healing. Gentle 'cross friction' massage to the tendon itself, relative rest, application of icepacks, ultrasound therapy and anti-inflammatory drugs are necessary additions. An injection of local anaesthetic mixed with cortisone may be recommended if the pain is marked.

Tennis elbow

Tennis elbow is a form of tendinitis on the outside of the elbow and forearm, affecting the upper end of the muscles which open the hand and straighten the wrist. Most people correctly diagnose their own tennis elbow.

Causes

Tennis elbow usually develops after repetitive and unaccustomed over-use, for example, after a long or hard game of tennis, using a hand tool such as a hammer or a screwdriver, or digging in the garden.

Initially there may be a transient ache that passes off. A few days later, when the arm is used, the pain reappears and persists for longer. Soon the arm cannot be used without pain. The condition is aggravated by any sort of gripping action. Even lifting a cup or plate can cause a spasm of pain, occasionally sufficient to cause the sufferer to drop the object.

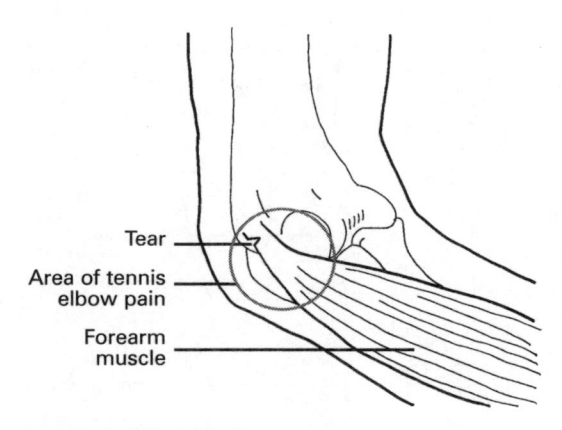

The location of tennis elbow

Treatment

Tennis elbow can be slow to heal, sometimes lingering for months, as it is difficult to sufficiently rest the arm. Treatment consists of gentle manual therapy, ultrasound treatment, avoiding sport, wearing a tennis elbow cuff, home application of heat balms, icepacks and anti-inflammatory drugs.

A cortisone injection may be recommended for a tennis elbow. This is usually more effective after manual therapy has reduced scar tissue and muscle tension. On rare occasions, an operation is needed if there has been a long history of symptoms which have not responded to the normal treatment methods.

Tenosynovitis

Inflammation of the inner lining of a synovial sheath (a slippery tube that surrounds a tendon to prevent it from fraying). A synovial sheath is present where a tendon bends round a corner and might fray, for example, at the wrist and ankle.

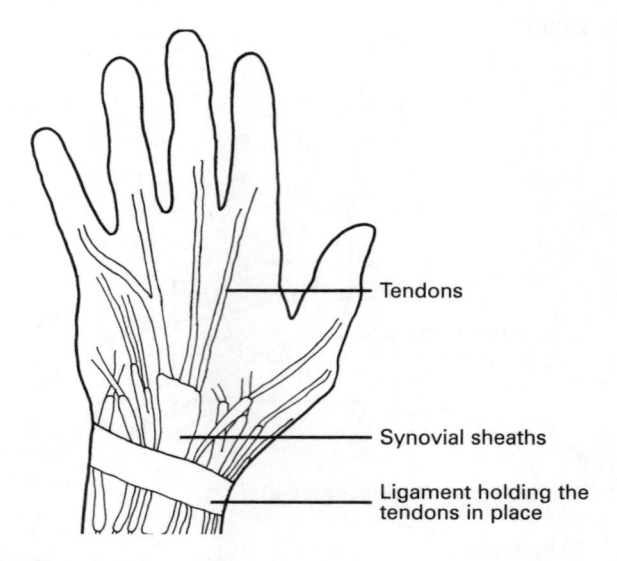

The wrist showing synovial sheaths

Tenosynovitis is usually caused by repetitive, unaccustomed over-use. Sport and activities such as using a paintbrush, a screwdriver or a hammer affect tendons in the wrist. In the ankle, running is the main culprit.

Symptoms include pain, tenderness and swelling over the tendon and spasm of the muscle attached to the affected tendon. Occasionally, a fine crepitus (sandpaper-like sensation) can be felt as the tendon slides through its sheath.

Treatment for tenosynovitis is similar to tendinitis, although the synovial sheath has a better blood supply and recovers more readily. Treatment includes gentle manual therapy, ultrasound treatment, application of icepacks and rest from aggravating activities. More severe cases might require an injection of cortisone.

Thumb pain

A thumb disorder is especially troublesome because the thumb is utilised in 90 per cent of hand activities. The thumb (thenar) muscles and the joint at the base of the thumb (carpo-metacarpal joint) are the most common sites of pain. It might be sprained, by the carpo-metacarpal joint being forced backward, or pain might develop with osteoarthritis. Manual therapy and anti-inflammatory drugs will resolve most cases. Sometimes an injection of cortisone is necessary when pain, tenderness and stiffness is severe or persistent.

Wrist sprain

Most wrist sprains are not severe. An X-ray might be advised to exclude the possibility of a fracture. Treatment follows the RICE rule: rest, ice, compression bandage and elevation in a sling. When more severe pain has reduced, gentle exercises and manual therapy may be recommended.

CHAPTER SEVENTEEN

LEG PAIN

- Ankle sprain ■ Anterior thigh pain
- Calf pain ■ Foot strain ■ Groin pain
- Hip and buttock pain ■ Knee pain
- Metatarsalgia ■ Posterior thigh pain
- Shin pain ■ Sprain

Ankle sprain

An ankle sprain is one of the most common injuries, comprising almost one-quarter of all sporting injuries. Going over on the outside of the foot usually causes the sprain and damages ligaments on the outside of the ankle. Sometimes a chip of bone can be pulled off with the ligament injury.

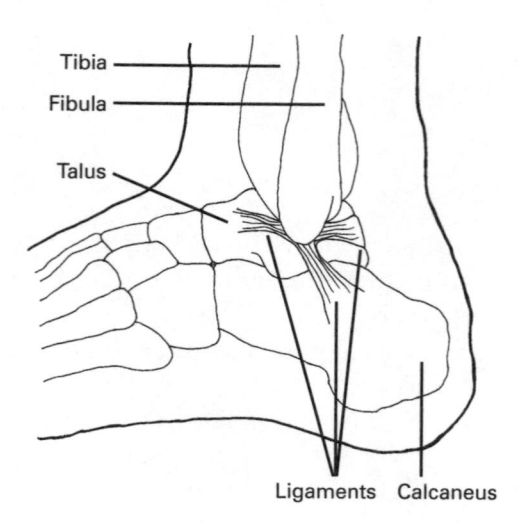

The components of the ankle joint

Treatment

First aid includes application of an icepack, a compression bandage and rest with the foot elevated. Early treatment, given within the first few minutes, will minimise swelling and bruising, and greatly shorten recovery. A severe sprain might require an X-ray to check whether the ligament has been stretched or ruptured, or the anklebone fractured.

Crutches may be needed for several days. Other treatments include wearing an elastic bandage or brace, anti-inflammatory drugs (aspirin-like medication), continued use of icepacks, ultrasound, manual therapy and exercises.

Anterior thigh pain

The anterior thigh contains the large, powerful quadriceps muscle that straightens the knee.

Causes

There are several reasons for anterior thigh pain. A contusion (bruising), sometimes called a 'cork thigh', and a haematoma (a collection of blood) are both caused by a direct blow to the thigh, often through playing body contact sports. Strain and rupture of the quadriceps muscle occurs during explosive muscle contraction like sprinting, jumping and kicking. The pain of a rupture usually settles quickly. If the knee is straightened after the swelling has subsided, the person notices a hollow (the rupture) in the thigh adjacent to a lump of shortened muscle.

However, the most common causes of anterior thigh pain, and probably more frequent than all other reasons put together, is pain referred from a back complaint. Less often, pain might be referred from the hip joint in conditions like osteoarthritis.

Treatment

Immediate treatment for a quadriceps injury is RICE (rest, ice, compression and elevation). Later, ultrasound, stretching, graded exercise and gentle massage can be introduced.

For pain referred to the anterior thigh, treatment is directed to the cause. The great majority of back problems that refer pain to the anterior thigh respond to manual therapy.

Calf pain

The calf extends from the back of the knee to the heel. It consists of two muscles, the gastrocnemius and the soleus, which join at their lower end to form the Achilles tendon that connects them to the heel. Contraction of the calf raises the heel at the same time as pushing down the ball of the foot. This is an essential action in walking, running, jumping and hopping.

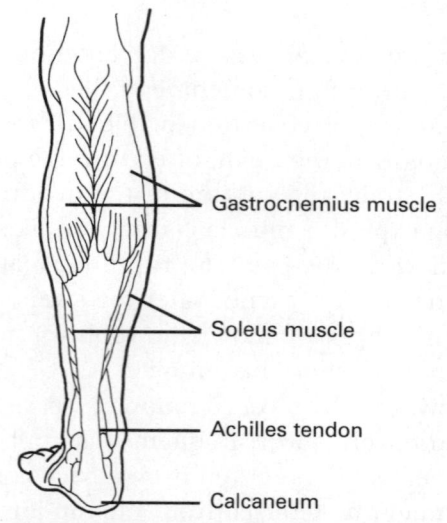

Calf muscle is composed of gastrocnemius and soleus muscle joining to form the Achilles tendon.

Calf pain can occur due to cramp (temporary lack of blood flow), calf muscle strain and sciatica (irritation of the sciatic nerve). Achilles tendinitis (inflammation of the tendon) affects the tendon joining the calf to the heel. Deep vein thrombosis and intermittent claudication (pain brought on by walking due to the narrowing of arteries and insufficient blood flow) are occasional causes of calf pain.

Each condition requires individual treatment. Manual therapy gives good results for cramp, muscle strain, sciatica and Achilles tendinitis. Other treatments might include ice-packs, ultrasound and stretching exercises. Medical advice is necessary for thrombosis and claudication.

Foot strain

Foot strain (also known as flat feet and claw foot) is an injury to the joints and ligaments in the middle part of the foot.

Causes and treatment

Arches that are abnormally low (flat feet) or high (claw feet) may be incorrectly blamed for the development of foot strain. However, foot strain develops in feet with any height of arch, including those with normal arches. The arch is not the reason for foot strain.

Unaccustomed running, walking, standing for long periods — such as when you start a new job, or spend the day shopping or sightseeing — can bring on foot strain. It might result from the rapid increase in weight during pregnancy or when marked weight loss causes the joints and ligaments of the foot to have less padding. The foot usually aches when standing, particularly underneath, and is only relieved by sitting down.

Manual therapy and stretching exercises will loosen stiffness, while strengthening exercises need to be performed in feet which are too mobile. Sufficient recovery time and rest from weight-bearing is necessary. A podiatrist can make moulded orthotic supports to redistribute body weight more evenly over the foot.

Groin pain

This is pain in the crease between the lower abdomen and front of the thigh. In males, groin pain can include radiation into the testicle.

Causes

Groin pain is a common symptom with a number of causes. It can present a diagnostic and treatment challenge for the unwary.

The back is the most common cause of pain in the groin. When present, it is referred from the region between the chest and lower back. Any sort of mechanical problem in this part of the spine can refer pain to the groin.

In athletes, the muscles in the lower back can be so over-developed and strong that they behave like a splint or corset. This adds strain and overloads the region further up the back, which in turn refers pain to the groin. (See Chapter 1, Predisposing conditions — adaptive stiffness.) Muscle spasm in the iliopsoas (the muscle that bends the hip and lifts the knee) can refer pain to the groin.

Local causes of groin pain can include strain, often during sport, of a muscle on the inside (adductors) or front (rectus femoris) of the thigh, inguinal hernia, osteoarthritis and hip joint disease.

Less often, groin pain might be due to kidney disease, urinary tract infection, stress fracture of the neck of the femur (top end of the thigh bone) osteitis pubis (inflammation at the pubic symphysis) and a pinched nerve in the front of the groin.

Treatment

Treatment of groin pain depends on the cause. Tests such as X-rays of the pelvis, hip or spine might be required.

Manual therapy is most effective for the common causes: referred pain from the thoraco-lumbar spine (junction between the chest and lower back), iliopsoas spasm and muscle strains around the groin. When a stiff lower back leads to overload and strain of the thoraco-lumbar region, manual therapy is also directed to the lower back.

A muscle strain on the inside of the thigh is treated with cold packs, ultrasound, massage and gentle stretching exercises. An arthritic hip may require anti-inflammatory drugs (aspirin-like medication), physiotherapy and exercises. Medical advice is necessary for non-mechanical causes of groin pain such as hernia, urinary tract infection or hip joint disease.

Hip and buttock pain

The hip joint is an extremely strong ball and socket joint. Stout ligaments and the most powerful muscles in the body surround it. It is remarkable that the hip joint is not injured more often because of the enormous strains and leverages put through it. It has to support the weight of the upper body and take the strain of running, lifting and all manner of strenuous activity. Fracture of the neck of the femur (upper end of the thighbone) is more frequent than a strain of the hip joint.

Causes

Most people who experience pain in the buttock or side of the hip think they have arthritis, which will ultimately require an arthroplasty (joint replacement).

Fortunately the back is the most common cause of hip

pain. The large majority of those with pain in the hip, buttock or groin have referred pain from a mechanical disorder in the lumbar spine rather than the hip.

Osteoarthritis of the hip joint can give groin pain that radiates down the front of the thigh. Placing stress on the joint, for example when reaching down to put on socks, will aggravate it. In children, causes of hip pain include Perthe's disease (damaged blood supply), slipped epiphysis (injury to the growing area of bone) and irritable hip (inflammation).

Treatment

Tests such as X-rays may be necessary to identify the problem and allow treatment to be directed to the cause. Manual therapy and exercises are the preferred treatment for the majority of those whose hip and buttock pain is referred from the back.

Anti-inflammatory drugs (aspirin-like medication) might be prescribed for osteoarthritis of the hip joint. Other measures might include manual therapy (massage and stretching), exercises (land and water), application of heat, weight loss and sitting down rather than standing when possible. Arthroplasty (joint replacement) is available for severe pain and disability.

Medical advice is necessary for other diseases of the hip.

Knee pain

The knee joint combines mobility with considerable strength and stability. Very strong ligaments on both sides and within the joint supply the strength. The latter are the cruciate ligaments, which may require 'reconstruction' when ruptured. In front, a huge muscle, the quadriceps, forming the front of the thigh, straightens and supports the knee. The patella (kneecap) is a bone embedded in the tendon, which allows the tendon to pass around the lower end of the femur (thighbone) without fraying. Two menisci (discs of cartilage) help distribute the body weight and prevent excessive pressure.

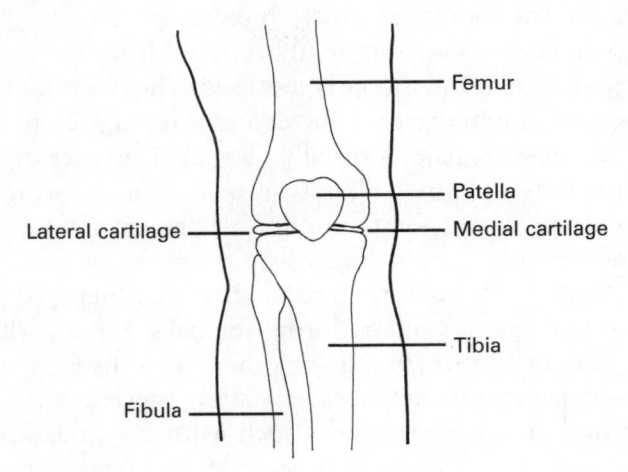

The knee joint

Causes

The knee is a complicated piece of machinery and a host of things can go wrong with it. We are always hearing of athletes in every field of sport who have injured their knees.

Twisting while bearing weight on the knee may injure a ligament or tear a meniscus. Repetitive overuse through activities such as running may cause tendinitis (inflammation of the tendon) below the patella or behind the knee. Knock-knee and bowleg are non-painful, temporary deformities in childhood, which usually disappear as growth continues. Active children can develop Osgood-Schlatter's disease (inflammation of the bony prominence below the knee). Recurrent dislocation or partial dislocation of the patella tends to occur in teenage girls. Chondromalacia patella (wear behind the patella) is a common source of anterior knee pain in young adults. Osteochondritis (traumatic injury to the articular surface of the thighbone) produces persistent pain and swelling. Bursae (fluid filled sacs) around the knee may become inflamed by local pressure, such as kneeling. Last but not least, the knee is a common site for osteoarthritis in older age.

Knee pain is also commonly referred from the back and hip joint. It is felt as a poorly localised ache, without tenderness, over the front of the knee, and is often present at rest.

The cause of pain is usually identified by careful assessment and testing, including X-rays. Sometimes, arthroscopy (inspection of the joint through a fibre-optic telescope) is necessary to confirm a diagnosis.

Although manual therapy is the treatment of choice when knee pain is referred from the back, it is usually only one part of the treatment for other knee disorders. Other measures might include icepacks, strapping, supports and/or crutches, electrical treatment such as ultrasound, strengthening exercises and advice on care of the knee.

Metatarsalgia

This is pain under the ball of the foot in the region of the metatarsal bones.

Causes and symptoms

Metatarsalgia is brought on by unaccustomed standing and walking. Pain develops in the small lumbrical muscles between the metatarsal bones or the ligaments binding the metatarsal heads together. Occasionally, a neuroma (benign tumour of the nerve) between the metatarsal bones causes metatarsalgia and a tingling feeling that spreads into the toes.

The sufferer has pain on standing, particularly when they first stand up in the morning or after sitting down. There is tenderness under the ball of the foot, usually worse between the second and third metatarsal bones. The joints of the midtarsis can be stiff and the calf muscle tight.

Pain area of metatarsalgia

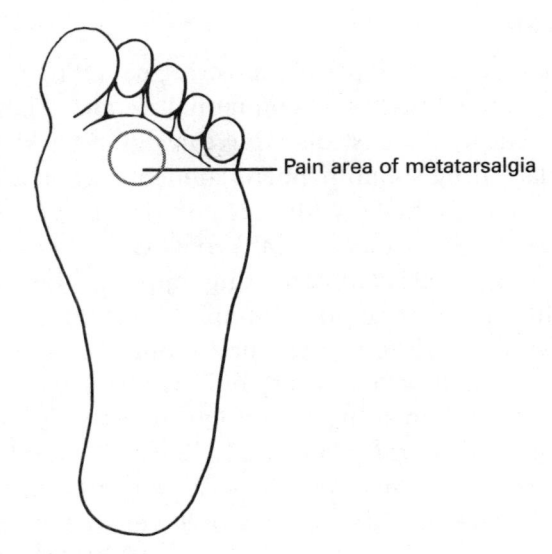

Location of the metatarsalgia

Treatment

Manual therapy usually gives excellent results for metatarsalgia. Treatment is directed to relaxing the lumbricals (small muscles between the metatarsal bones), loosening the mid-tarsus and, if necessary, the rest of the foot and calf.

Ultrasound is also useful, and people may be advised to limit standing or walking. Mobilising (loosening) and stretching exercises can help. A metatarsal pad from a pharmacist or an orthotic support made by a podiatrist might take the pressure off the mid-tarsis and offer a solution.

A neuroma usually requires surgical removal when there is persistent tingling and pain into the toes.

Posterior thigh pain

The posterior thigh contains the big group of hamstring muscles that bend the knee and swing the leg backwards at the hip.

Causes

There are three types of hamstring pain. Firstly, sprain of the hamstring muscles is common in sport. Tight hamstrings prevent footballers following through after kicking the ball. A hamstring sprain happens suddenly when a runner accelerates or gradually with repeated strenuous exercise.

Secondly, a mechanical problem in the lower back can prolong a persistent hamstring injury. In this case, the hamstring pain is mild, grumbling, recurring and poorly localised, with tenderness and reduced capacity to stretch it out. There is also a history of lower back pain.

Finally, hamstring pain might be entirely due to a lower back mechanical problem. It is usually milder, without a sudden onset and poorly localised, and the sufferer has lower back pain or a history of lower back trouble.

Treatment

The immediate treatment for a torn hamstring is rest, ice, compression, elevation and gentle stretching. Later on, ultrasound and graded massage can be introduced, followed by strengthening exercises and a return to increasing activity.

Manual therapy plays a greater role in recovery if a hamstring injury is slow to recover or becomes a chronic, grumbling problem. When a lower back problem is detected, treatment is directed to both the hamstring and lower back.

Shin pain

Shin pain, or shin splints, in the front of the lower leg between the knee and foot is a common complaint among athletes. It is brought on by excessive and unaccustomed walking or running that damages the shin muscles. There are five types of shin splints including myositis (inflammation of a muscle), tendinitis (inflammation of a tendon), periostitis (inflammation of the bone where the muscle attaches), and occasionally, a stress fracture; the fifth, a rare but serious type of shin splint called anterior compartment syndrome (build-up of pressure in a muscle), is a medical emergency. An operation is needed to decompress the shin muscle and prevent it from dying.

Treatment

Treatment is directed to the cause. An X-ray or bone scan might be needed if a stress fracture of the tibia (shinbone) is suspected. Rest from the activities that aggravate the pain will often clear up the shin splints in a few weeks.

If the pain is more marked, use of icepacks, ultrasound, and a course of anti-inflammatory analgesics (aspirin-like medication) might be necessary. Otherwise, manual therapy with stretching exercises is effective, particularly in chronic or recurring cases.

In rare cases, an operation is needed to release severe inflammation pressure within the muscle (anterior compartment syndrome), as it would otherwise die for lack of circulation.

Sprain

A sprain (also known as ligament injury and joint sprain) is a tearing or overstretching of a ligament or joint capsule caused by a sudden pull or strain. Ligaments connect the bones and are the restraining harness that prevents a joint from moving too far. The capsule is a thinner membranous bag that encloses a joint and produces the synovial fluid that keeps joint surfaces moist and slippery.

The most commonly sprained ligaments are at the ankle and knee. The degree of damage varies from a few torn fibres (first degree), a stretched ligament (second degree) to complete rupture (third degree).

Sprain leads to swelling of a joint, which cannot be moved without aggravating the pain. There may also be spasm (involuntary contraction) of surrounding muscles to splint and protect the injury.

First aid treatment consists of RICE (rest, ice, compression and elevation). An X-ray may be necessary to exclude a fracture. First- and second-degree sprains are treated with ice, bandaged support and rest. As pain subsides, they can be given gentle manual therapy, ultrasound and exercise.

A third degree sprain (ligament rupture) should be immobilised in plaster or repaired surgically, followed by use of a limited motion brace.

Chronic sprain

Chronic sprain refers to sprain of scar tissue (inelastic fibrous bands of collagen) left behind from an earlier injury. Ankle injuries frequently leave residual stiffness and lead to a chronic sprain.

Scar tissue slightly shortens the natural length soft tissues, making them less pliant and prone to future damage. The story of Graham in Chapter 1, Collagen, the body's glue, is typical of a chronic sprain. An old ankle injury with scar tissue is repeatedly re-injured, leading to further scar tissue.

Manual therapy is particularly beneficial for a chronic sprain. Massage and mobilisation help to halt and reverse the continued production of scar tissue and stiffness, and restore pain-free mobility. Exercises are also prescribed to help restore strength, mobility and balance.

FINDING YOUR MANUAL PRACTITIONER

CHAPTER EIGHTEEN

- Recommendation ■ The telephone book
- Making a phone call ■ Approach treatment sceptically ■ Assess the rate of progress

These days, many people have become discerning, critical and sophisticated observers of the various professionals who supply their health services. They have realised that they are entitled to clear and accurate information, to dignity, to privacy and to appropriate time. They want their healthcare professionals to support their well-being and offer prevention as well as cure.

Healthcare is about more than just technical knowledge and processes. It concerns people and human relationships. It's about trust, empathy and support. This means that a professional who works well with one person may not be right for another.

When we choose our healthcare professionals, we assess their professional quality and their 'fit' for our own needs. We apply the same criteria to manual practitioners. If anything, consumer power is even more important here because the choice of manual practitioner is wide.

Recommendation

The best place to start is with a direct recommendation. This often comes from a family member or a friend who is enthusiastic about their own therapy or who notices that your symptoms are similar to theirs, or that it sounds like a manual problem. Ask several of your friends and see if any one name keeps cropping up. When two or more people recommend the same person, like many things in life, you can be reasonably confident that you are on the right track.

Quiz your informants thoroughly; they can be helpful but sometimes prejudices can keep you from the right person. How experienced is the practitioner? Did they say sensible and logical things about what was wrong? Did they give an indication of how many visits it would take and what might be done if there was no progress? Are they fair-minded towards colleagues and other professions?

More and more, medical practitioners are recommending manual therapy. But you may find that their views lean more towards those branches of manual therapy that they know most about and are aligned with conventional medicine, such as physiotherapy. You should question your doctor about his or her choice, as you should for any referral.

Ask your doctor for a list of options rather than a single name. Ask whether manual physiotherapy or massage, or an osteopathic or chiropractic approach, might be better or worse, and if they know of a practitioner with a good reputation. Ask your doctor about the practitioner who interests you and whether he or she has had any feedback from other patients about that practitioner.

Your local pharmacist, as well as dispensing helpful medication, may be a good adviser. They often listen to their customers' health problems and solutions, and may be able to recommend a good manual practitioner for you to see about your particular aches and pains.

The telephone book

Business directories (yellow, pink, private or public) record the names of masseurs, osteopaths, chiropractors and manual physiotherapists. Make a list of those you can conveniently reach.

Research their abilities by asking around. Friends, work colleagues, even friends of friends, local pharmacists or a medical practitioner can all be useful. Don't be put off by sweeping generalisations about a complete profession. Individual people, their reputation and skills are much more important than the profession they belong to.

Notice the kind of company they keep. You may prefer a manual practitioner who works closely with conventional doctors; you may like one who shares premises with alternative practitioners like naturopaths. Both are useful clues to their approach.

Making a phone call

Ring the prospective practitioner and ask them about your problem and whether it is something they treat and have success with. If you can't get through because they are busy, ask when would be a convenient time to speak to them. A good practitioner will ask intelligent and logical questions and perhaps offer recommendations for initial home treatment and they won't be pushy about making an appointment. They should not sound unduly evasive or exaggerated in their claims. They should inspire confidence.

Ask about the cost, the length of the appointment, and the number of visits you can expect to make. Cheaper but shorter appointments can work out to be more expensive in the long run. Of course, price is not everything. What fixes the problem is the best value. A good reputation and integrity is much more important and will probably give you better value in the long run.

Approach treatment sceptically

You are most welcome to ask your manual practitioner for an assessment and opinion about the problem without receiving any treatment at all. You can always change your mind during the course of a visit once you are satisfied and more confident about the person, or you can go away and consider the advice before deciding what to do.

Remember that treatment is about a relationship, so you should listen to your own intuition. A good practitioner will give you confidence and the advice and treatment that he or she would wish to receive if they were the patient.

We know from research that people cannot easily differentiate between the quality of the actual service provided and the way the practice is presented. Only about half of the impression created is produced by the service. The other half is influenced by factors such as premises, furnishings, staff, attire, magazines, convenience, parking, how the practitioner and staff communicate, and even the toilets. Although these are indirect indicators of service, the client may or may not equate them with the real quality of the 'hands on' service actually given by the practitioner.

Assess the rate of progress

Progress should be clear-cut. Once the appropriate treatment has been identified, you should generally expect to improve at almost every visit. Even the most longstanding problem should show useful evidence of progress over three or four treatments. (See Chapter 4, Progress in longstanding problems.) The affected region should feel looser, the painful area become more localised and then more intermittent.

If improvement has stalled and you are not making further progress, ask what can be done about it. If the treatment path proposed does not lead to improvement, consider moving to another practitioner. Do not feel embarrassed about consulting somebody else. Seeking a second opinion is common practice in healthcare. There are plenty of other practitioners to choose from.

This does not mean the therapy already carried out has been of no benefit. It may have provided a solid foundation to build on. A fresh mind and treatment approach often brings excellent results and you will benefit by building on the previous therapy.

Resources

Association of Massage Therapists of Australia, 250 High Street, Prahran, Vic 3181. Phone: (03) 9510 3930. Fax: (03) 9521 3209. Email: amta@amta.asn.au Web: www.amta.asn.au

Association of Massage Therapists, Level 1, Suite 3/47 Spring Street, Bondi Junction, NSW 2022. Phone: (02) 9369 2998. E-mail: massage@amtnsw.asn.au Web: www.amtnsw.asn.au Includes web directory of practitioners.

Australian Association of Musculoskeletal Medicine. These are medical practitioners with a special interest in the non-surgical treatment of musculoskeletal problems. Most are general practitioners who can diagnose your problems and give manual therapy or, if the problem is more complex, recommend you to a suitable manual practitioner. Web: www.aamm.asn.au Includes web directory of practitioners.

Australian Osteopathic Association, Federal Office, PO Box 242, Thornleigh, NSW 2120. Phone: (02) 9980 8466. Fax: (02) 9980 8466. E-mail: aoa@tpgi.com.au Web: www.osteopathic.com.au Includes web directory of practitioners.

Australian Traditional Medicine Society, Unit 12/27 Bank Street, Meadowbank, NSW 2114. Phone: (02) 9809 6800

Chiropractors Association of Australia, National Headquarters: PO Box 6246, South Penrith DC NSW 2750. Phone: (02) 4731 8011 Fax: (02) 4731 8088 E-mail: nhq@caa.asn.au Web: www.caa.com.au Includes web directory of practitioners

Institute of Registered Myotherapists of Australia, PO Box 646, Carlton South, Vic 3053. Phone: 0500 500 646.

Massage Association of Australia, PO Box 1187, Camberwell, Victoria 3124. Phone: (03) 9885 1187. Fax: (03) 9532 4848. Email: info@maa.org.au Web: www.maa.org.au Includes web directory of practitioners.

Musculoskeletal Physiotherapists Association of Australia (Vic), Level 3, 201 Fitzroy Street, St Kilda, Vic 3182. Phone: 9593 8025 E-mail: margaret.grant@physiotherapy.asn.au Web: www.physiotherapy.asn.au Includes web directory of practitioners.

Queensland Association of Massage Therapists, PO Box 459, Springhill, Qld 4004. Phone: (07) 3236 9255 Email: qamt@nwi.com.au Web: www.qamt.nwi.com.au Includes web directory of practitioners.

Society of Clinical Masseurs, 1163 Burke Road, Kew, Victoria 3101. Phone: (03) 9817 7577. Fax: (03) 9817 7588. Email: societycm@bigpond.com Web: www.users.bigpond.com/societycm/ Includes web directory of practitioners.

GLOSSARY

Complementary practitioners Non-conventional therapists who can work alongside and in conjunction with medical practitioners.

Hard tissues The bones.

Hypertonia Raised muscle tone or contraction in response to an injury; less intense than muscle spasm.

Manual practitioners/manual therapists Practitioners of massage, chiropractic, musculoskeletal physiotherapy, osteopathy and manual medicine.

Manual therapy Hand treatment of musculoskeletal disorders.

Mechanical disorder Any condition that responds to manual therapy.

Medical practitioner A doctor with a degree in medicine.

Orthodox/traditional medicine Conventional mainstream medicine.

Palpation The process of examining by means of touch.

Reflex An automatic response to a stimulus that is transmitted by the nervous system. For example, muscle spasm is an involuntary response to a pain stimulus.

Soft tissues Any of the five tissues that connect the bones — muscle, fascia, ligament, joint capsule and disc.

Subluxation The chiropractic name for a mechanical disorder.

Thoracic vertebra One of twelve spinal vertebrae between the neck and lower back.

Viscera Any of the organs situated in the chest and the abdomen — heart, lungs, liver, digestive tract, etc.

INDEX

abdominal functional disturbance 34, 53, 194–7
acromio-clavicular (AC) joint strain 213–14
activator technique 89, 95
acupressure 89, 92–3
acute torticollis (wry neck) 187–8
adaptive stiffness 24
adjustment 88–9
adolescent kyphosis 203
aging 25–6
anger 175
ankle sprain 226–7
annulus fibrosis, sprain of the 148–50
anterior thigh pain 227–8
applied kinesiology 96
arm pain 213–25
aromatherapy 84–5
arthritis of the spine 164–5
articulation (stretching) 86–7

basic insight 9–10
basic techniques 5
blurred vision 169–70
body framework 38–40
bone 38–9
  disease 71
'bone out of place' 69–73, 155–8
bonesetters 97–8
Bowen technique 85
brachial neuritis (brachialgia) 188
bursitis 214–17

calf pain 228–9
cartilage 39–40
cervical
  headache 180–4
  ribs 189–91
  sprain 191–3
chest wall pain 198–200
chiropractors 53, 58, 103–6, 116–19
chronic sprain 238
coccydinia 204–5

collagen 18–20, 81
concentration, poor 175–6
contraction headache or cervical headache 180–4
crack, the 76–8, 88
cracking joints 136–8
cranial manual therapy 94–5
curvature of the spine 161–4

degenerative arthritis 140–4
diagnosis 41–5, 78–80
disc 38, 81
  bulge 148–9
  degeneration 153–5
  herniation 151
  narrowing 153–5
  prolapse 151
  protrusion 151
  slipped disc 148–50, 151
  sprain 148–50
  thinning 153–5
disease 23–4
dislocations 216–17
double diagnosis 55–7

ear symptoms 167–9
earache 167–8
education 125–6
emotional stress 26–8
exercise 89–91
eye symptoms 169

facet joint strain 155–7
fascia 36, 81
fatigue 26–8
finger sprain 216–17
foot strain (flat feet, claw foot) 229–30
fracture and dislocation 216–17
friction 84
frozen shoulder (adhesive capsulitis) 217–19
functional disorders 34, 52–3, 126

golfer's elbow 219
groin pain 230–1
growing pains 138

hard muscle spasm 13
hard tissue 9
headache
  post-traumatic 173–4
  tension 180–4
heavy arm syndrome (T3 syndrome) 200–1
hip and buttock pain 231–2
inhibition 83–4
injury
  previous 22–3
  sports 25
intervertebral disc problems 147–8
intervertebral joint strain 155–7
joint sprain 237–8
joints 73–6
  capsule 37–8, 81
  cracking 69–80
  disfunction 178–9
kneading 83
knee pain 232–4
leg pain 226–38
ligament 37, 81, 237–8
longstanding problems 64–7
manipulation 88, 128
manual medicine 107–8, 119–20
manual physiotherapy 108–9, 120–2
manual practitioners 239–43
manual therapy 1, 2–3, 5, 6, 9–10, 53–4, 58–60, 80, 110–12, 122–4, 171–3
  advantages 28–31
  and bone disease 71
  claims 126
  cranial 94–5
  current medical attitude 132–4
  dangers 127–9
  education 125–6
  how it works 12–15
  placebo effect 127
  unprofessional behaviour 129–31
  unproven science 124–5

massage 82–6, 98–9, 112–14
  sports 84
mechanical diagnosis 43–5
mechanical disorders 9, 10–12, 49, 51, 54–5
mechanical sinus pain 177
medical attitude, current 132–4
medical diagnosis 41–2
medical diseases 54–5
metatarsalgia 234–5
migraine 125, 171
mild depression 174
minimising reactions 67–8
misalignment 155–7
misdiagnosis 57–8
mobilisation 87, 120
muscle 33–4, 81
  contraction headache 180–4
  energy technique 93–4
  spasm (hypertonia) 13, 24, 138–40
musculoskeletal system 8
nerves 40
  trapped 46–8, 208
oesophageal (gullet) pain 201–2
osteoarthritis 140–4
osteoarthrosis 140–4
osteochondritis 202–3
osteopathy 53, 58, 100–1, 101–3, 114–16
pain 15–16, 170
  anterior thigh 227–8
  arm 213–25
  calf 228–9
  chest wall 198–200
  groin 230–1
  growing 138
  hip and buttock 231–2
  knee 232–4
  leg 226–38
  mechanical sinus 177
  oesophageal (gullet) 201–2
  posterior thigh 235–6
  referred 48–9, 170
  shin (shin splints) 236–7
  shoulder 220–1

sinus 176–7
thumb 225
pain–spasm–pain cycle 16–18
percussion 84
physiotherapy, manual 108–9, 120–2
placebo effect 127
polarity balancing 85–6
posterior thigh pain 235–6
post-traumatic headache 173–4
postural strain 158–9
predisposing conditions 21–8
pregnancy and the back 160–1
psychological symptoms 174–6
reactions 61–3
  minimising 67–8
  unusual 63–4
referred pain 48–9, 170, 210
reflex effects 50–1
reflexology (zone therapy) 86
reiki 85
relaxation (Swedish) massage 84
remedial (therapeutic) massage 84
resources 243–4
respiratory restriction 202
rheumatism 140–4, 164
Rolfing or postural integration 85
rounded back 202–3

sacroiliac joint strain 206–7
safety 6
scalenous syndrome 189–91
scar tissue 19, 22
scepticism 67
Scheuermann's disease 202–3
sciatica 207–9
scoliosis 161–4
shiatsu 89, 92–3
shin pain (shin splints) 236–7
shoulder pain 220–1
sinus pain 176–7
  mechanical 177
sinusitis 176–7
slipped disc 148–9, 151
snoring 178

soft tissues 9, 12, 81
  diagnosis 32–45
  injury 144–5
somatic dysfunction 155–7
spinal degeneration 164–5
spine disorders 147–65, 186, 194
spondylolisthesis 211–12
spondylolysis 209–11
spondylosis 164–5
spondylosis deformans 164–5
sports
  injuries 25
  massage 84
sprain (ligament injury, joint sprain) 225, 229–30, 237–8
stress 64
stroking 83
subluxation 96, 145–6, 155–7
sway back 159–60

temporomandibular (jaw) joint disfunction 178–9
tendinitis 35, 220, 221–2
tendon 34–5, 81
tennis elbow 222–3
tenosynovitis 223–4
tension headaches 180–4
thoracic
  outlet syndrome 189–91
  spine and chest 194–203
thumb pain 225
tinnitus 168–9
traction 91–2
trapped nerves 46–8, 208
treatment
  methods of 81–96, 98
  responses 61–8
trigger points 89, 92–3
twitching (flickering) eyelid 170

unprofessional behaviour 129–31

vertigo (giddiness) 184

whiplash 191–3
wrist sprain 225
wry neck 187–8

X-rays 71, 73, 131–2